DOUGLAS ATWILL
PAINTINGS

DOUGLAS ATWILL
PAINTINGS

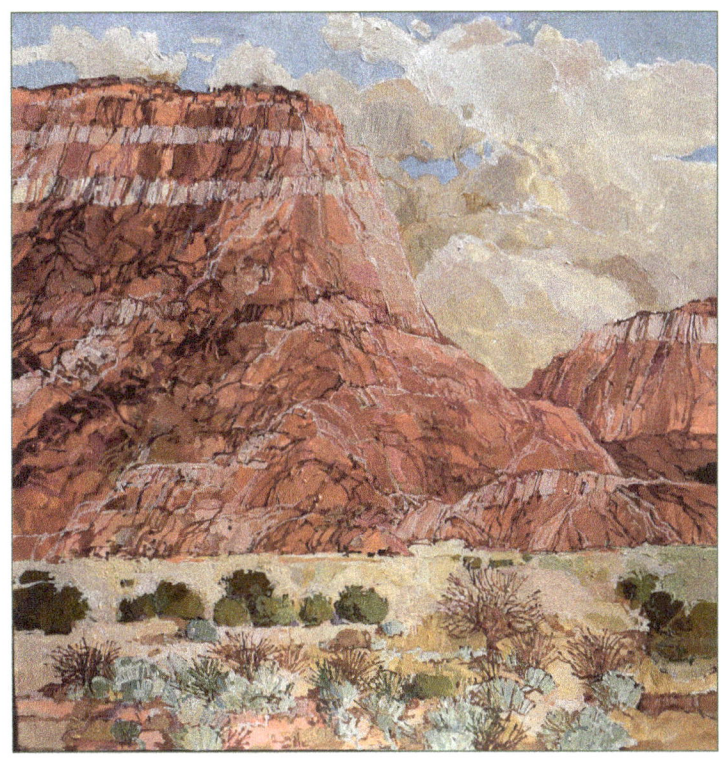

DOUGLAS ATWILL

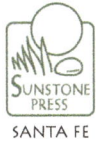

SUNSTONE
PRESS

SANTA FE

Sunstone books may be purchased for educational, business, or sales promotional use.
For information please write: Special Markets Department, Sunstone Press,
P.O. Box 2321, Santa Fe, New Mexico 87504-2321.

Body typeface › Poliphilus Pro
Printed on 70 pound acid-free paper

Library of Congress Cataloging-in-Publication Data

Atwill, Douglas, artist, author.
[Paintings. Selections]
Douglas Atwill paintings / by Douglas Atwill.
pages cm
ISBN 978-0-86534-841-7 (softcover : alk. paper)
1. Atwill, Douglas--Themes, motives. I. Title.
ND237.A826A4 2015
759.13--dc23
2015026199

WWW.SUNSTONEPRESS.COM
SUNSTONE PRESS / POST OFFICE BOX 2321 / SANTA FE, NM 87504-2321 /USA
(505) 988-4418 / ORDERS ONLY (800) 243-5644 / FAX (505) 988-1025

This book is dedicated to Victor L. (Pete) Stewart.

Preface

At the suggestion of Jim Smith at Sunstone Press, I have put together this small book with photographs of a group of my paintings accompanied by some thoughts about them. It is not intended to be a fine, thick-papered catalog but rather an informal gathering of some work from recent as well as earlier years. Jim said that with the new digital scanning and printing, it was possible to print quite good reproductions without the hire of a museum curator, light-tables and color charts.

With a few exceptions, the paintings are of landscapes or gardens. These have been my motifs since moving to Santa Fe nearly fifty years ago. The early landscapes were mostly set in the Galisteo Basin or up in the Sangre de Cristo mountains, places that were readily available to me. The Galisteo paintings were often started as *plein-air* canvases but finished in the studio because of a rising wind or a sudden threat of storm. More than once my canvas and easel went bouncing off in a strong gust.

My eye usually went to the long lines of color across the basin— bands of color across the horizon, alternating between terracotta-red cliffs, the varying green clumps of pinons or chamisa, and vast patches of ochre-yellow grasses.

The mountain scenes came from hikes along the Big Tesuque stream with my German Shepherds Annie and Sister. After their initial tentative splashings in the stream, the girls invariably led me to the water motifs. Even in late winter, with patches of snow on the north slopes, there was an endless variety of water, rocks, trees, willows and grass combinations. Sketches and photographs became the source materials that I still use today, often seeing new ways to use them.

In the late 70s I built a house in Galisteo village on property that Betty Stewart and I bought from Jose Ortiz y Pino. Betty restored the stone ruin on her half and I designed a house facing south into a walled garden on my side. The large living room worked perfectly as a studio and allowed me to take breaks from painting by tending the adjoining espalier trees and perennial borders. I lived in Santa Fe and commuted the half-hour out every day—the opposite direction from most Galisteo villagers. Early morning light across the valley gave many ideas for the Galisteo motifs.

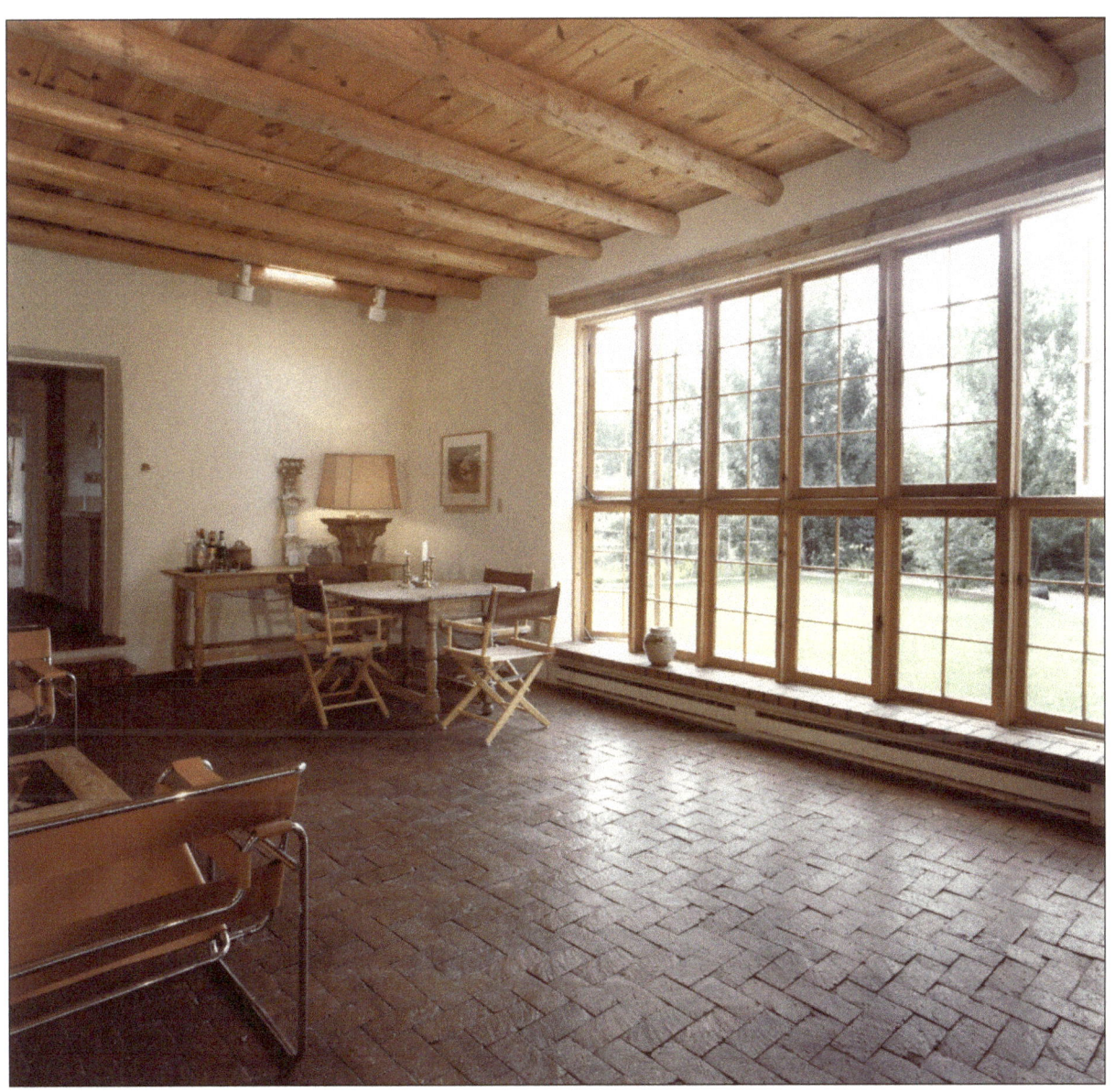

Now years later, I am building another new studio on Cristobal Lane in the Museum Hill area of Santa Fe. It will stand a short distance away from the house and have the same south-facing light as the Galisteo studio, and a long window on the north for the cooler light. The balance been the two light sources has been something I learned to appreciate in the many studios intervening.

I have drawers full of landscape photos taken over the years, a rich trove of sources for my new work. I search through them with an older sensibility, looking for different patterns and ideas from the younger painter who took them. And some new trips to Galisteo and the Big Tesuque are called for....chancing that no quick windstorm will upend the easel and/or the painter.

There will be a new garden on Cristobal Lane, not so extravagant as my earlier gardens. It will certainly contain an herbaceous border with daisies, poppies, coreopsis, lavender, delphinium, peonies and spring bulbs. I will repeat the great success from the last garden, a grid of 64 lavender plants in homage to the fields of the south of France. The latilla/coyote fencing around the garden will be a perfect backdrop for climbing roses and espaliered semi-dwarf apple trees. And clumps of lilacs, forsythias, kolkwitzias, plums, apricots, aspens, and horse-chestnuts will fill out the corners. All will be watered by a hidden drip system, giving bounty with a minimum of water.

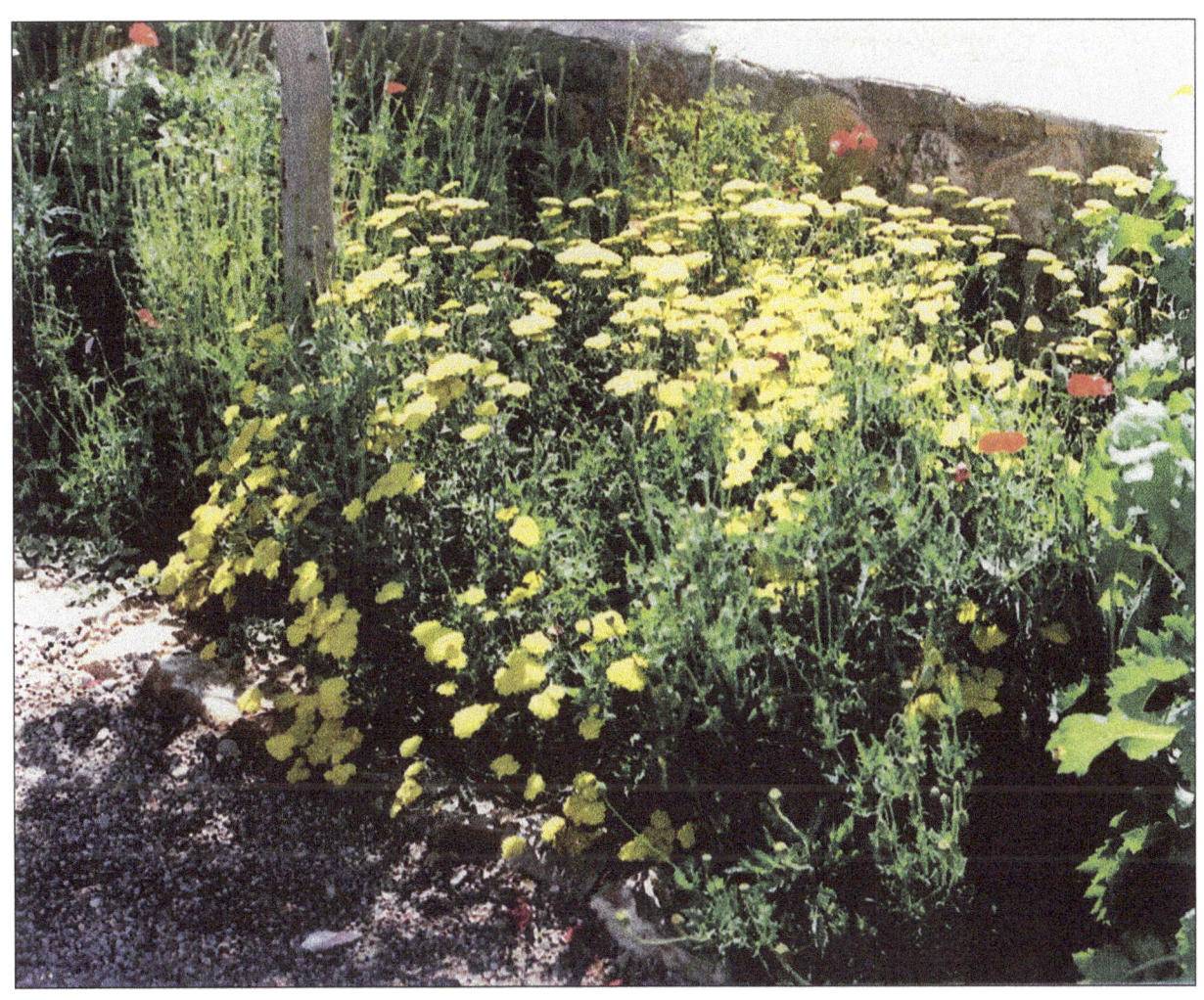

In the early years I preferred the almost-square format for a painting....slightly higher on the vertical dimension, such as 32x30 or 44x40 or 58x54. To most eyes it appeared to be square, but with an odd strength. Now I have taken to the exactly square or strongly rectangular. I have tried long horizontal shapes but they often seem contrived.

I have mixed brands of acrylic paint without worry, long preferring the water-based paints to the oil paints of old. The areas of flat color that now find their way into my canvases are easier to create with acrylic paints. Although missing the subtle quality of glazing that oil paints offer, I find other ways to make gradations in tone and color. And acrylic paints, unlike the linseed oil based paints, seem to be the right medium for artwork done in the 21st century.

The land around Black Mesa is an iconic scene that stays on my mind, perhaps fuelled by images of the events that ensued there during the Pueblo Revolt of 1693. And farther north the brick-red and white escarpments of Abiquiu are up for newer and different versions.

There are places I want to return to for photos and sketches. The Bosque del Apache never disappoints, and the Diablo Canyon can be attractive at any season. La Bajada hill is a strong motif at most times of day. The Black Canyon of the Gunnison River is a recent discovery for me and I expect some more paintings from there.

I spent a summer month in Maine on the Penobscot Peninsula years ago and would love to return there for new *plein-air* work. Asking each night at dinner to see what I had painted that day, the other guests at

Minerva's Folly purchased nearly all of the forty or so canvases. I have none left for this book.

I work at the easel almost every morning, three to four hours with the telephone and doorbell interruptions ignored. When everything goes well—the hand, eye and mind all working in concert—there is no happier day. It is now a good year when I am able to complete thirty-five to forty paintings, what I used to do in a month. Most mornings are without background music, but the Saturday opera broadcasts from the Met can effectively rush things along.

My painting table scares some people because it seems in such disarray, tubes left without caps and brushes marinating in opaque gray water. A tidy, well-pressed woman visitor to my studio years ago said such sloppiness was her worst nightmare. But it pleases me enormously, and I can find whatever color I want in a second or two. My new studio will have a separate storage room for the odd canvases that build up— half-finished portraits, abstract experiments and imaginary scenes that did not work out. Perhaps I should make a bonfire of them, but instead they remain as a silent testament to my ill-taken forays. There are times, however, that a new path can lead to a happy end.

Among the motifs that I've taken up and in the end abandoned are the salt marshes of South Carolina. I suppose it was the linear quality of the marshes that caught my imagination—stripes of yellow-green grasses alternating with the colors of still water. They could have been a watery version of the bands of color I saw in Galisteo.

A 1982 winter trip with friends to Egypt inspired several dozen paintings, most of the Nile and the dry desert beyond. The painters of our travel group—Walter Cooper, John Fincher, Forrest Moses, and me—had an almost sell-out Egypt exhibit a year later at the old Munson Gallery by the Compound Restaurant. There were enough canvases left over for me to have a solo show at the Dubose Gallery in Houston the next year. I would like to go back to the Nile, drift slowly by the temples and antiquities with sketchbook and camera. With the troubles there I doubt it is possible now.

Separate trips over the years to Norway, France, Greece, Spain, Turkey and Morocco all gave a harvest of paintings and a stack of pen-and-ink sketchbooks is all that remains. Morocco keeps returning in my mind. It must be the similar colors and shapes there to ones in New Mexico, red escarpments and rocky streambeds, desert and water intermingled, and the crumpled evidence of orogeny everywhere.

The white-washed villages of the Aegean islands continue their call, too. If the world has become more unsettled, how appealing is a high village of thick-walled houses clustered together way above the dark waters below? What could be a better symbol for safety in an unsafe world—a protected, tightly-packed village away from pirates attacking from the sea and the sound of falling governments?

Recently, I went with friends on small ship going up the Danube and then down the Rhine. I had visited most of the river towns in my 1957-58 Army years, so I spent the day on the deck sketching India-ink scenes of the towns, cliffs and vineyards. There probably will be no paintings resulting from these sketches but they have improved my sketching hand. We talk about a similar trip down the Rhone from Lyon to Avignon in the near future.

In the end, it probably does not matter what the motif is, if it shows the obsession of the painter. It is a great gift to be able to paint whatever you want and show it to the world. If Alexander Pope thought that true wit was "*nature to advantage dressed,*" then I might venture the same words as a succinct description for both garden and landscape paintings.

Tristan's Garden *30x30 Acrylic on Linen*

I was listening to the Metropolitan Opera's Saturday
broadcast when I started this painting, so I chose
Tristan as a title for this garden.
It is in truth my own garden with
one of the young horse-chestnut trees. I like to
include the suggestion of an adobe wall and the
mountain view, both of which can be seen
from most corners of the garden.

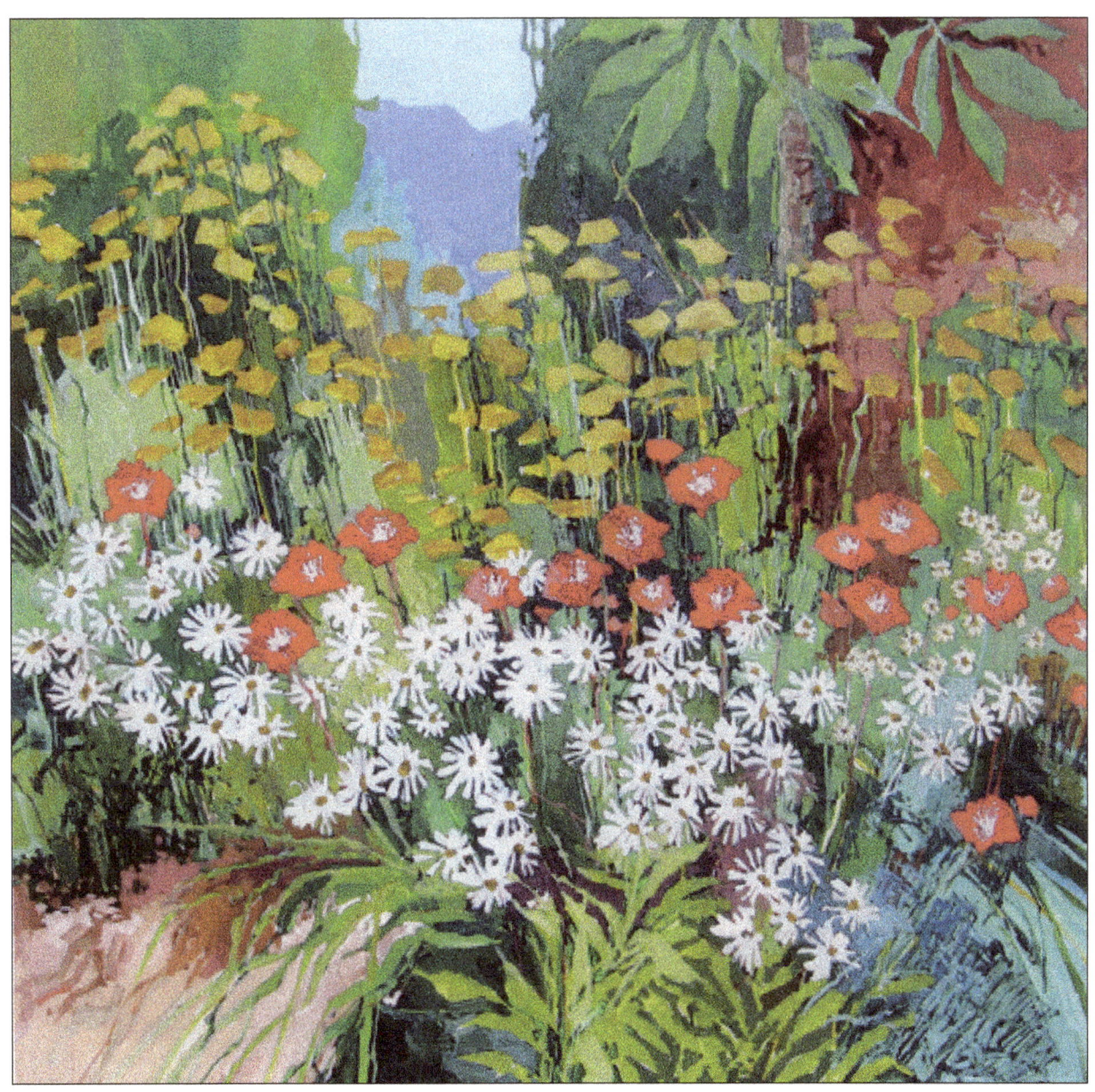

Eastview from the Creston, Galisteo *36x36 Acrylic on linen*

If you climb up on the Galisteo Dike, the one
just north of the village, this is the view
off to the east. Sometimes the water is visible in
the river, but this is a summer-without-rain version.
What has always interested me about the
Galisteo Basin are the layers of color that
delineate the landscape there. In the late afternoon, just
before the sun goes down, the lines of pinon and
juniper can appear almost black.

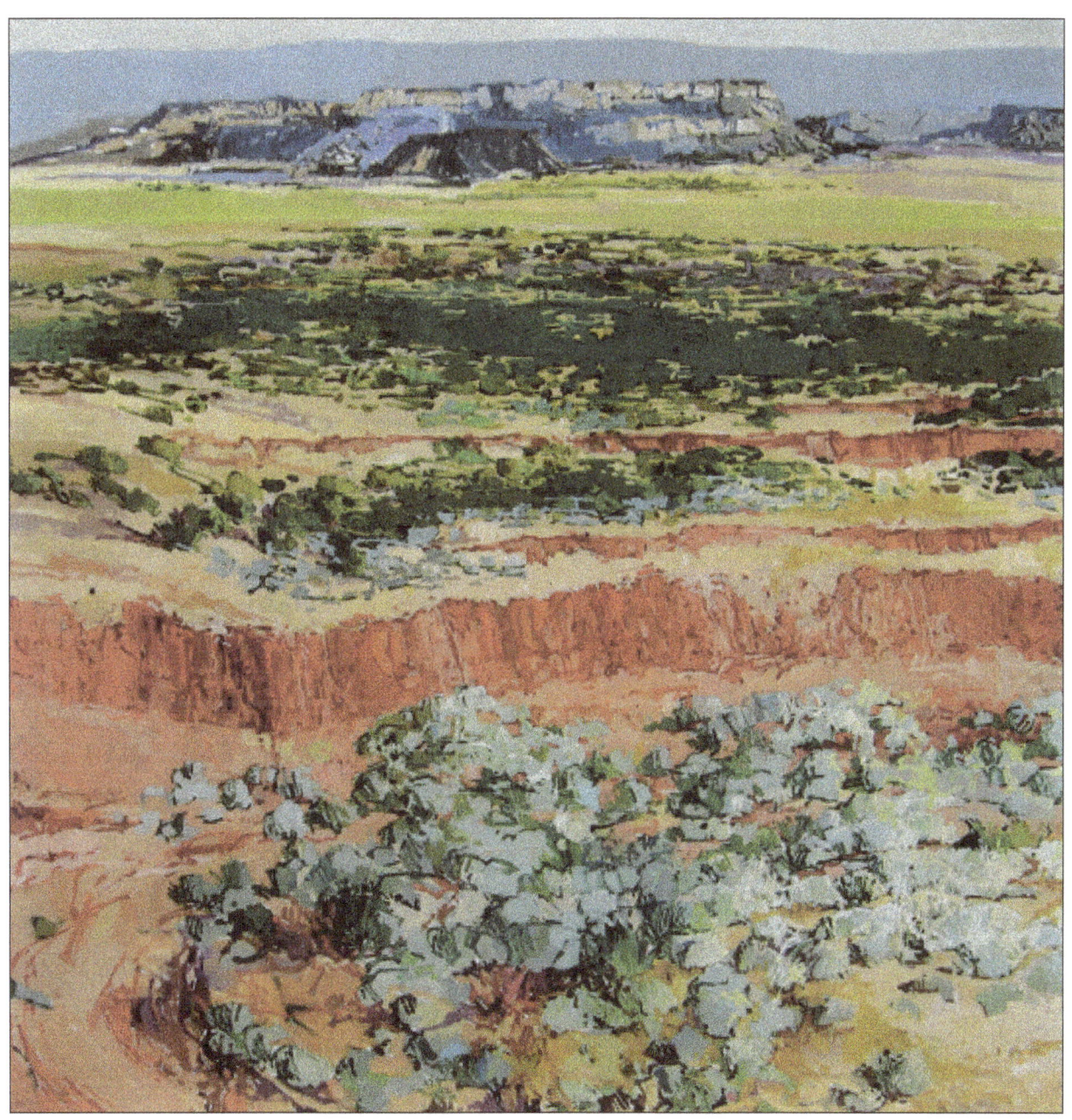

The Elektra Falls *54x44 Acrylic on linen canvas*

Another title from the Saturday opera,
this one thanks to Richard Strauss. In an odd way,
the sharpness of the music suited the subject.
This is a waterfall
on the way up to Lake City in Colorado,
properly called South Fork Waterfall,
off to the side of the road and
a grand surprise in the otherwise
flat and green valley.

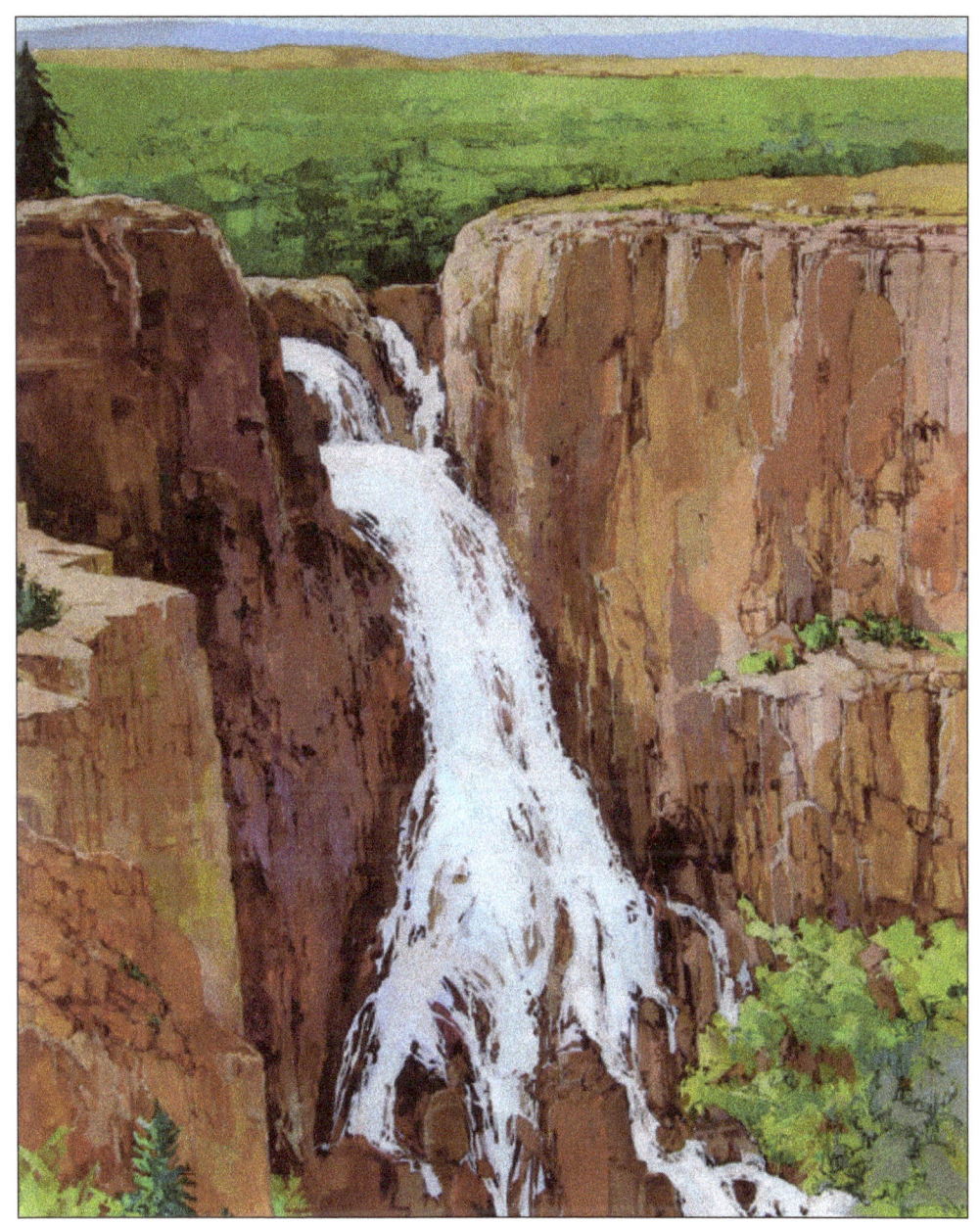

Black Canyon IX *24x24 Acrylic on linen canvas*

Unlike the horizontal sedimentary rock
formations of the Grand Canyon in Arizona,
the Black Canyon of the Gunnison
has almost vertical lines of a more ancient
rock. Not really black, but very dark in the shade
and warmer in the full sun. Set-designers for
tragic operas should
feel right at home here.

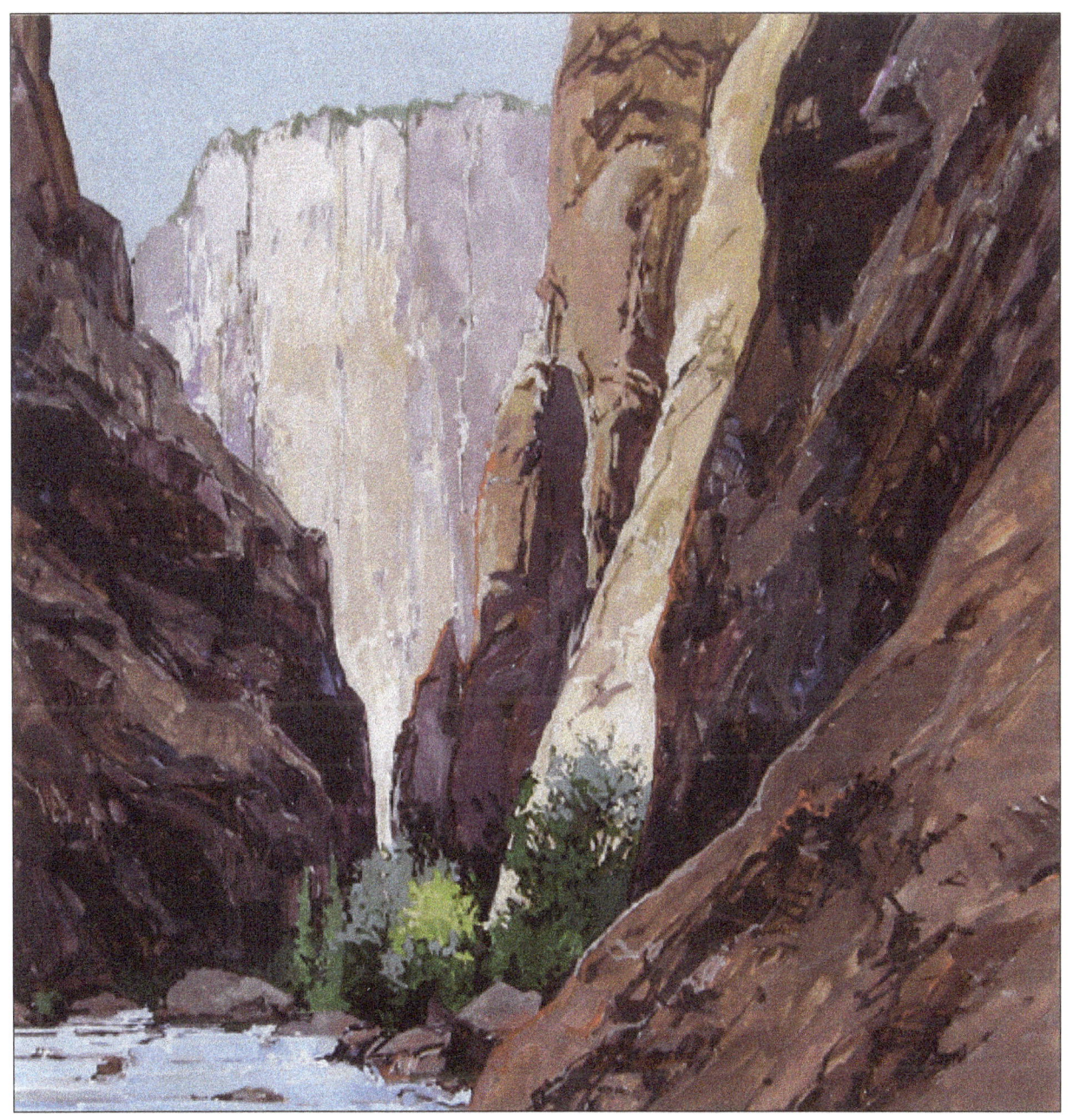

Fort Union Garden Autumn *58x54 Acrylic on linen canvas*

This is the second year of this garden,
the aspens making a good show of yellow,
crabapples and rose foliage in deep reds in
late September. The only
display of color from flowers is the Perovskia,
or Russian Sage—a lavender-like plant. I wanted this to
be a tapestry, flat colors making natural patterns
with just the barest touch of sky. The steps
suggest there is a way out.

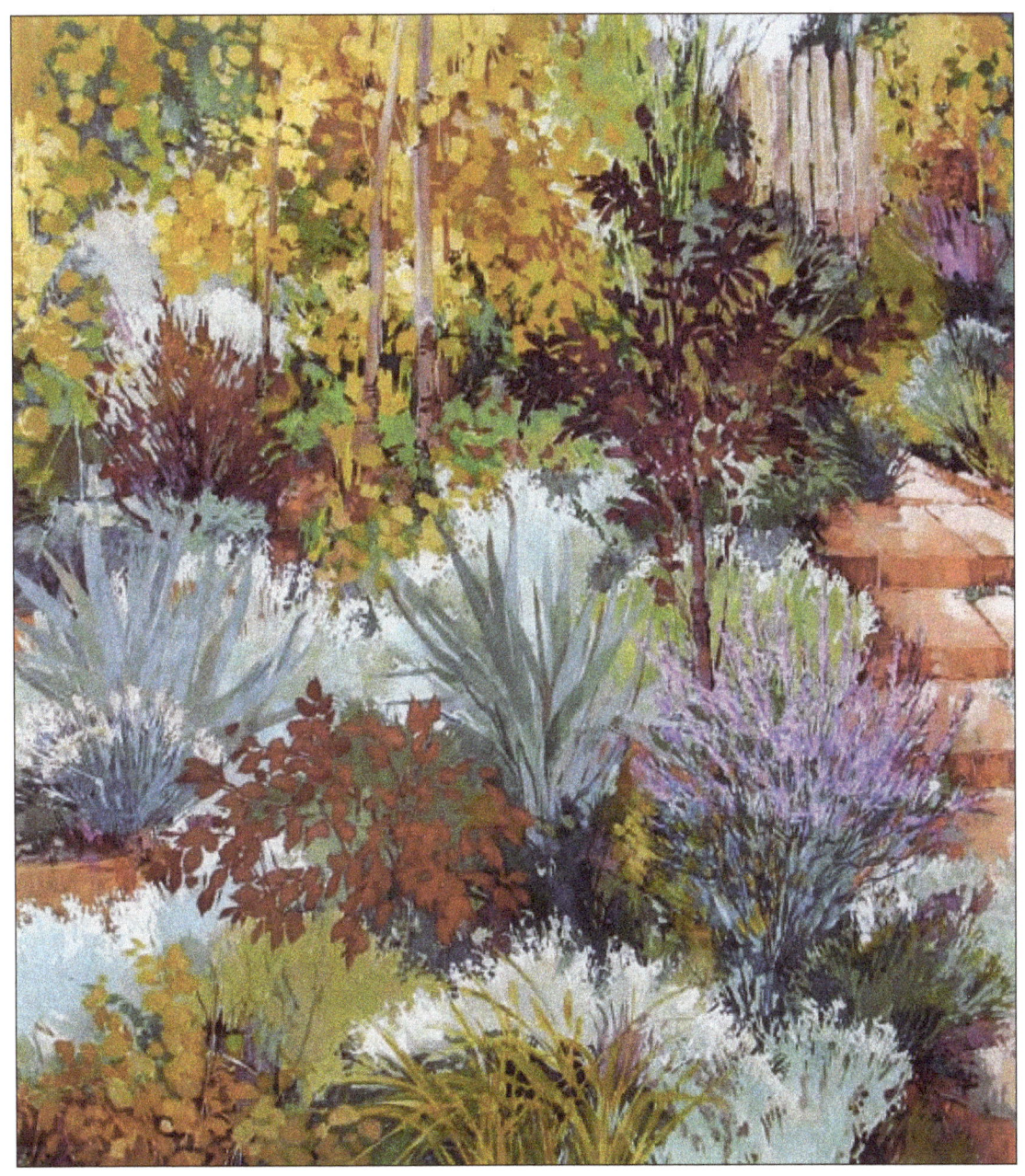

Fort Union Garden with Steps II *44x44 Acrylic on linen canvas*

A midsummer take on the same garden,
newly planted spring before last. In time,
I think the natural reseeding of
annual Flanders Poppies will become
more dominant and the yarrow just a
supporting color—the reverse seems to apply
in this version. Again, a contemporary
rendition of a *verdure* tapestry, overall pattern
more important than any individual plant.

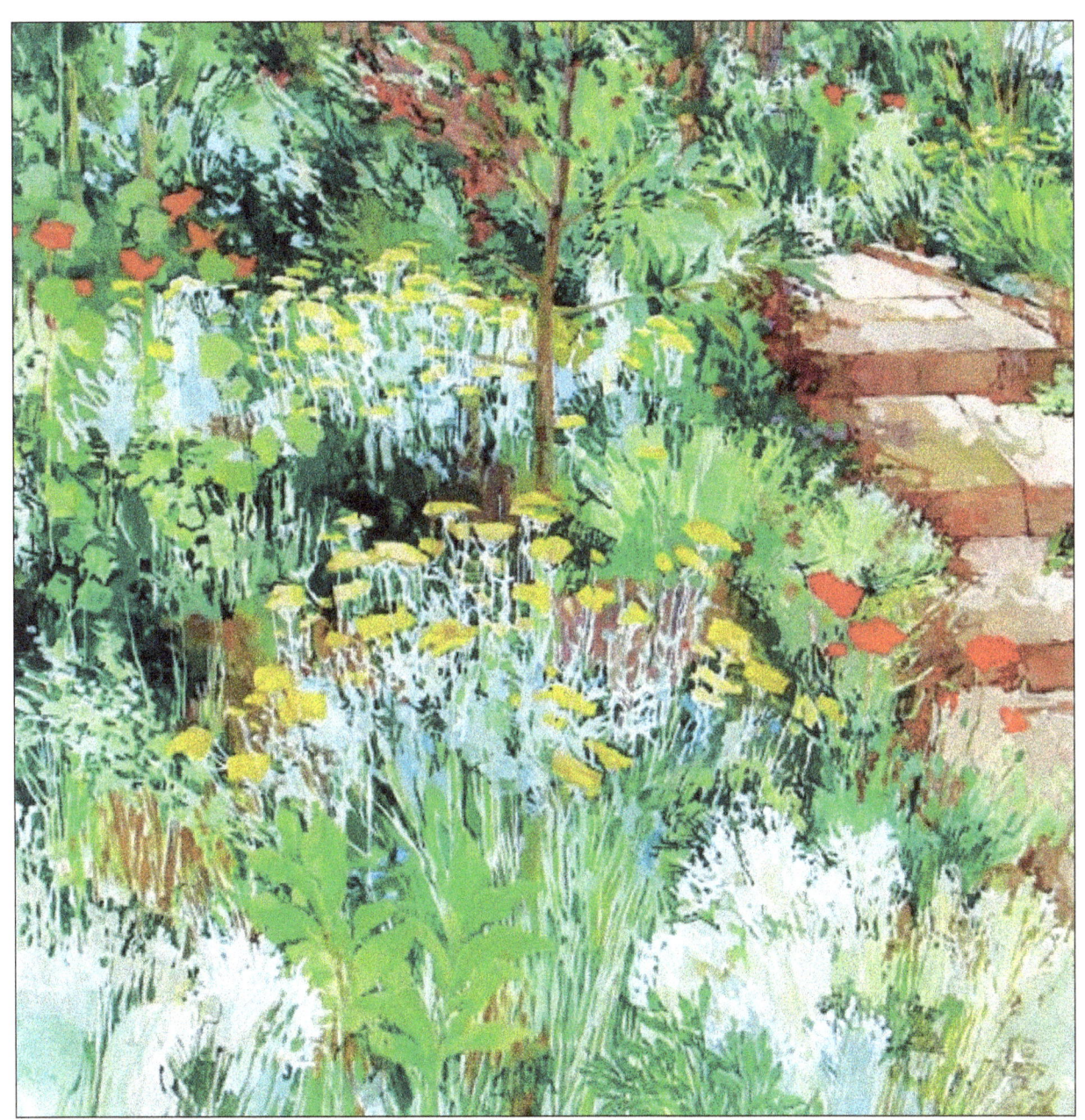

Turkish Tulips *30x30 Acrylic on linen canvas*

Against the adobe wall, the tulips have grown
tall and leggy, waiting for some rain and wind to
flatten them. I wonder if
another color, perhaps an earth pink
or deep violet would have been
better in this location. Yellow is predominant
in spring, however, and these chrome-yellow tulips
were chosen to work with a forsythia scheduled
to bloom on the other side of the garden.

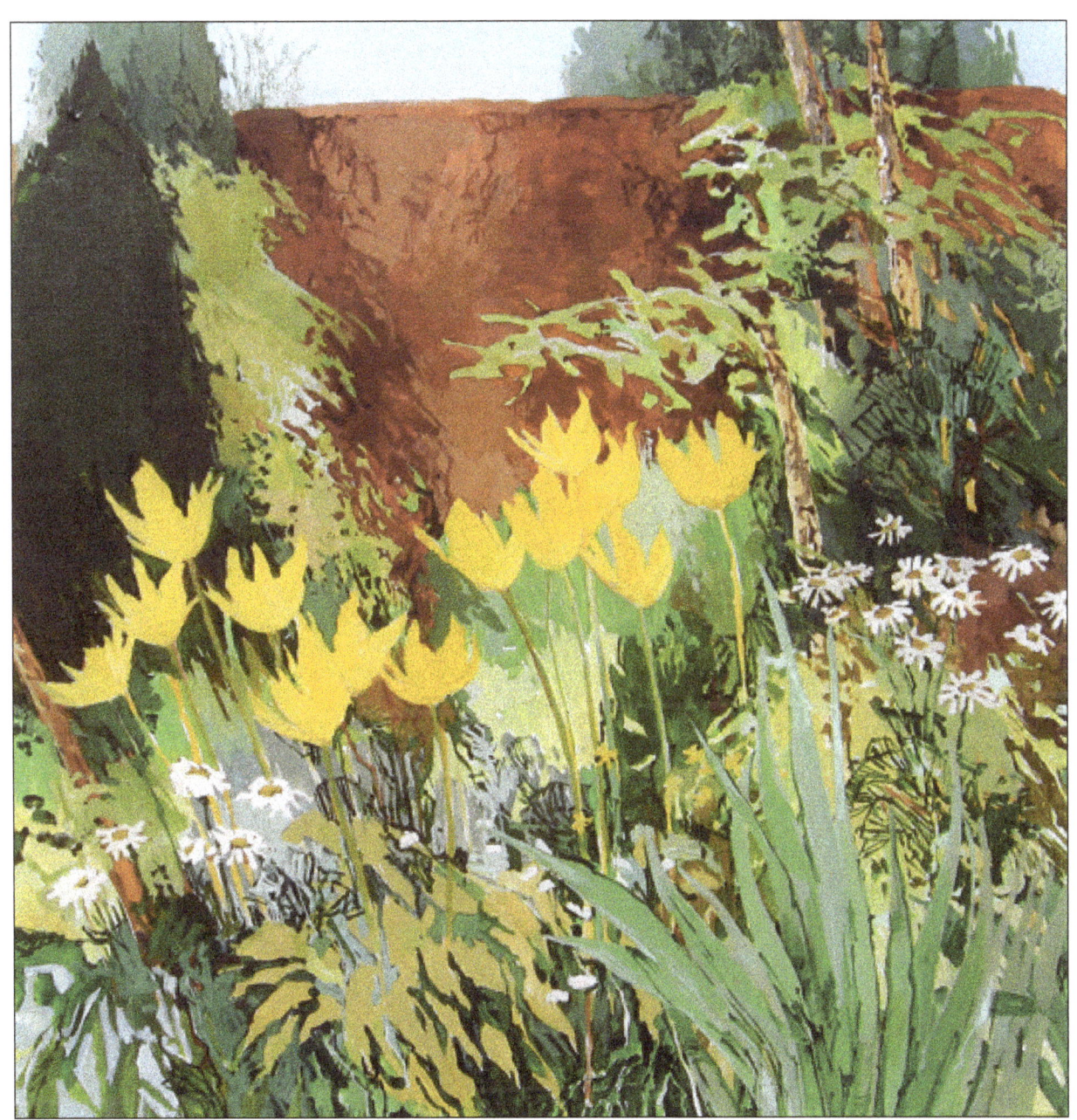

Barbados Garden *36x36 Acrylic on canvas*

For twelve years a group of friends and I rented
a house named Bluff House on Barbados, to hide away
from the wintry January of New Mexico. At first,
this enthusiastic Santa Fe painter took an easel and paints
into the sugar cane fields, coming back with a daily
canvas from the island interior. I hired an elegant
old Bajan man with his taxi to carry me out to the locations.
He waited for an hour or two, listening to island
cricket matches on the taxi radio
while I painted. On several days it started to rain, and
Mr. Paradise came unbidden with an umbrella, standing next to
me until the storm passed. After a few years of this, a certain
tropical torpor settled in and I chose to sketch
the villa garden from the shady verandah. This canvas
was painted back in my Santa Fe studio from one
of those sketches...tropical leaves parting to
give a glimpse of the Caribbean beyond.

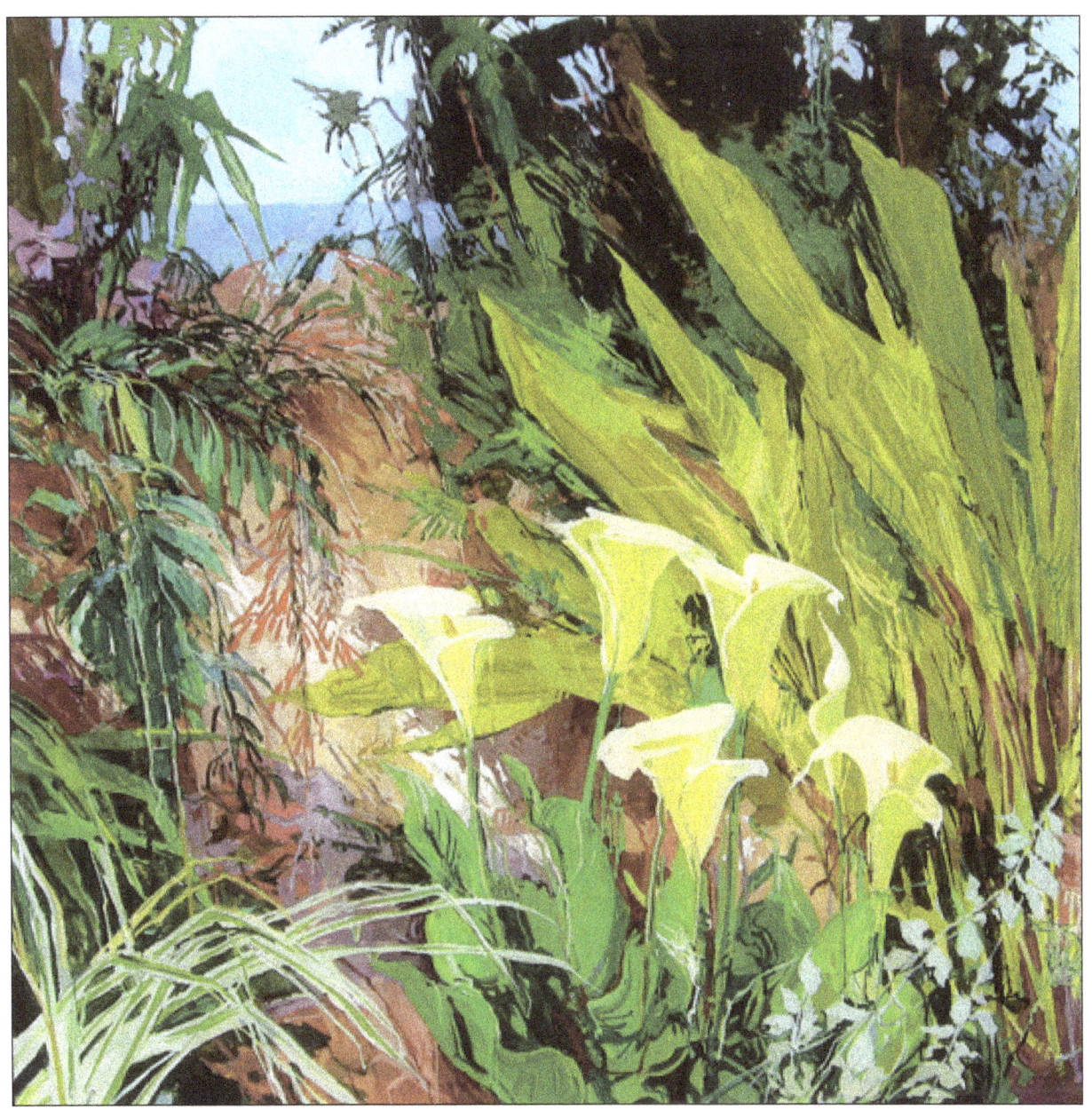

Apple Tree at Camino Rancheros Studio *12x52 Acrylic on linen*

We transplanted an apple tree from the far back
of the property at Camino Rancheros to a more salubrious
location just outside the French doors of the studio.
I had hoped we did not injure it in the process.
The next spring it signaled its approval by producing
many extra large blooms. It seemed only right
to record it with a painting.

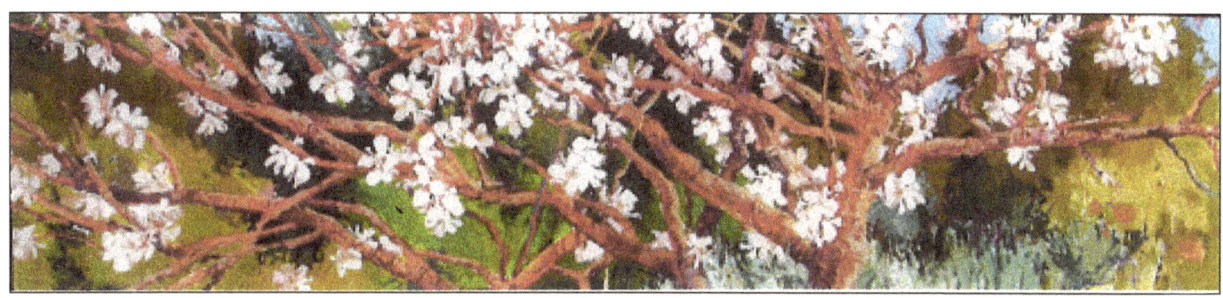

Escarpment Church II *18x18 Acrylic on canvas*

It is an odd juxtaposition, a small stucco church
in the New Mexico wilderness with a primeval
volcanic escarpment as a backdrop. For now, the
white, naïve purity is holding its own against the
sheer, dangerous bulk of the fiery rock.

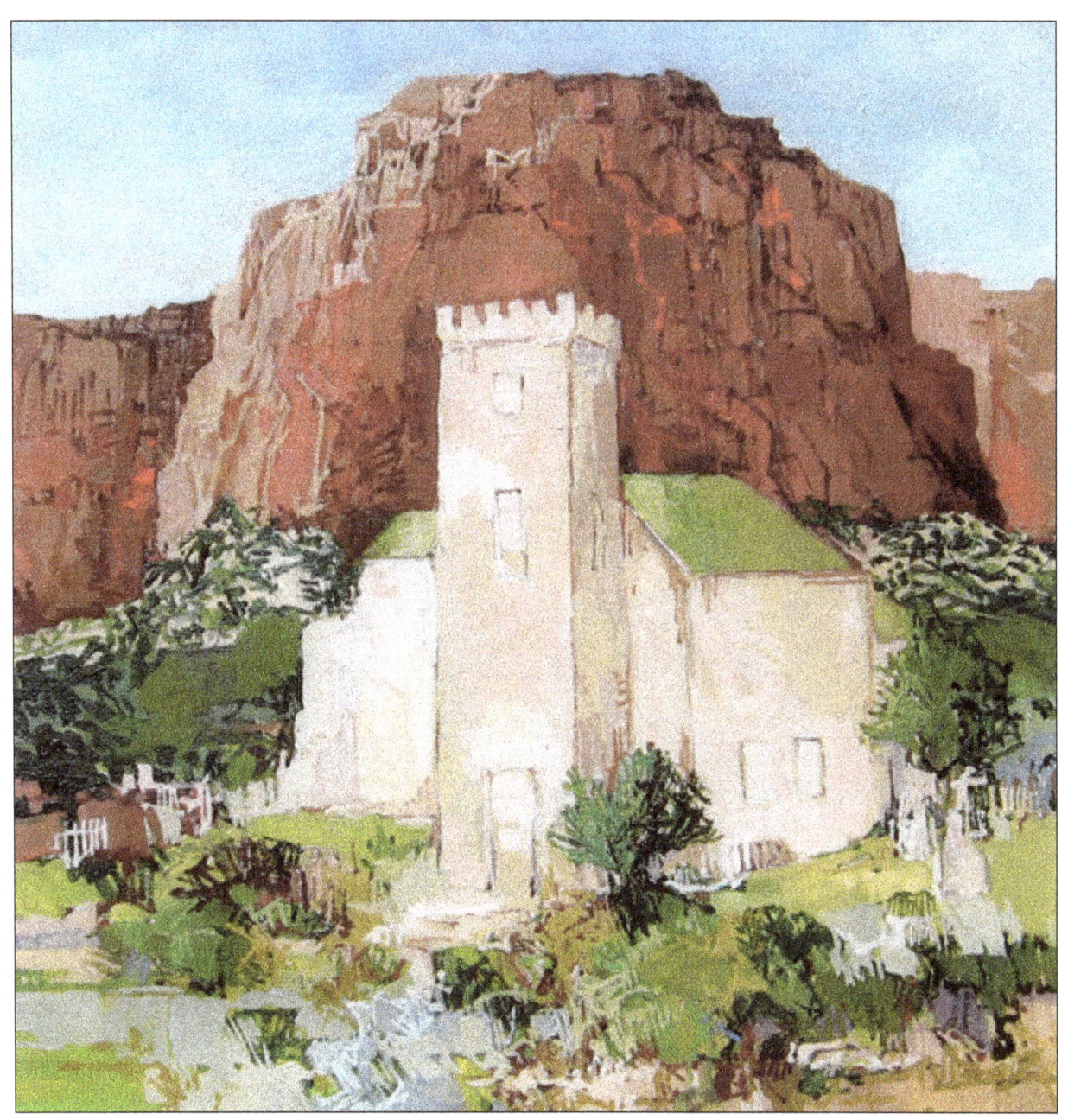

Summer Garden with Side Path *34x34 Acrylic on canvas*

This was the flower border at the Canyon Road studio,
the second year for the perennials with annual poppies
re-seeding here and there. Second and third year gardens
are often the best for painting,
everything at full tilt before the slow decline
in following years. The side path for me gives
a foil to the busy pattern of the plants.

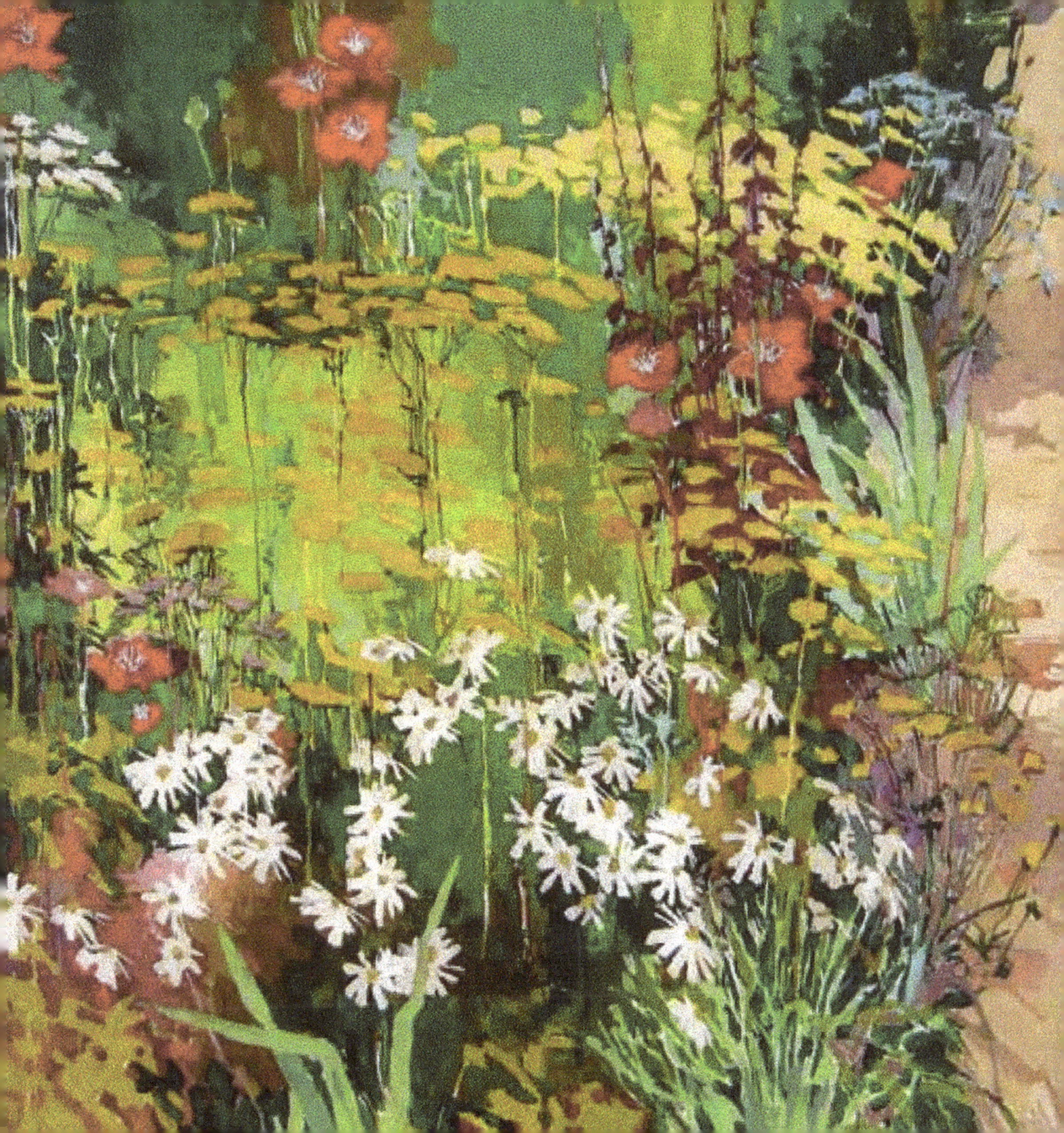

House with Palm, Tangier *44x44 Acrylic on linen*

We drove south out of Tangier towards the Atlas mountains,
headed for Ouarzazate and the desert. I remember this scene
along the way of a house in the hills but had no sketch
or photograph to document it. It stuck in my mind like a tune.
So I pulled it together from bits and pieces:
the palm from a painter's house in Le Cannet,
the aloe from a sketch along the Moroccan roadside
and the arched doorway from memory.
I keep working on it
when the occasion presents itself.

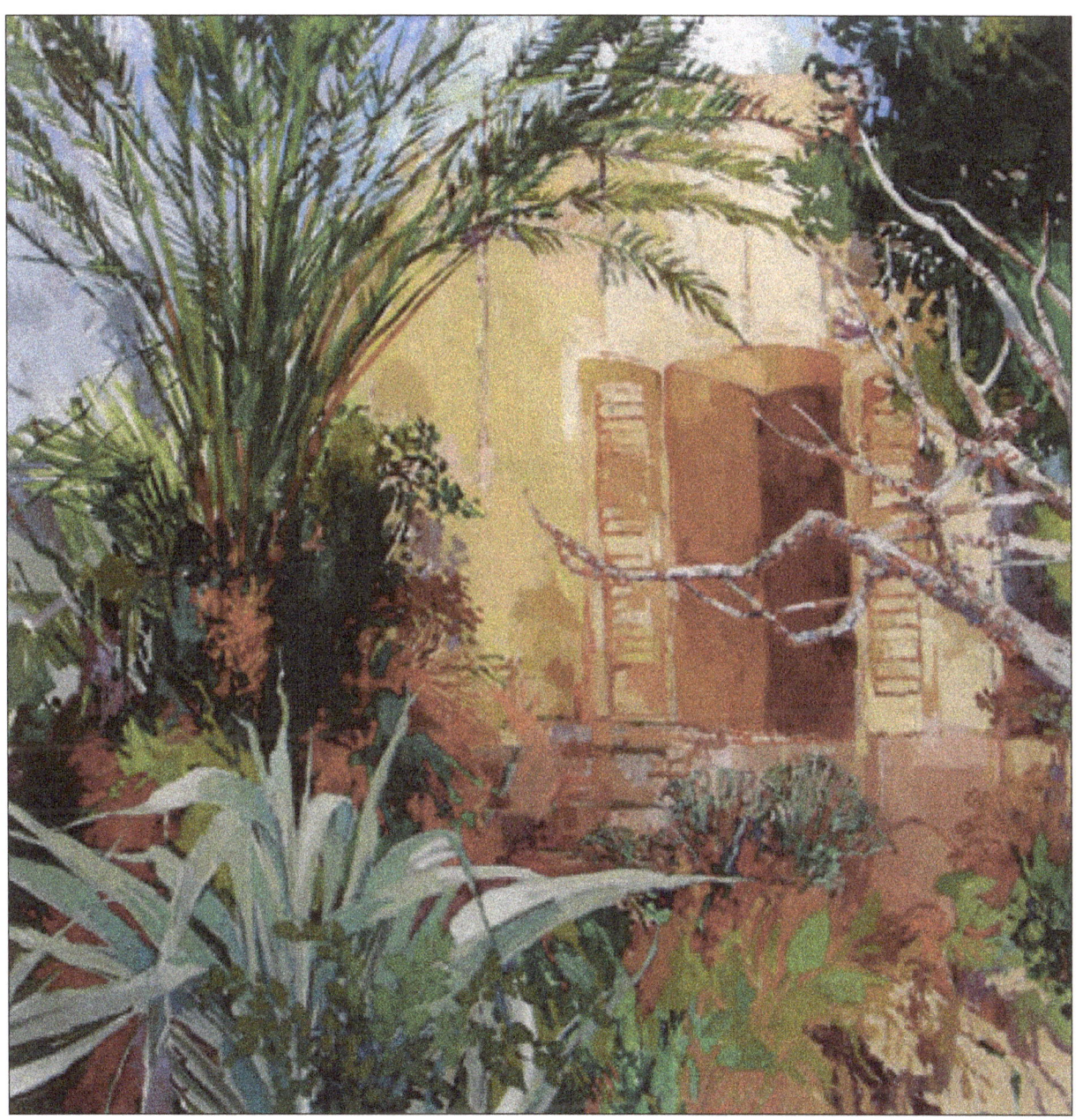

Sky Near Ortiz Mountains *24x24 Acrylic on canvas*

I am sure that the storm did not bring
any raindrops to the ground, but it was
an appealing image. It was painted from the west-facing
portal of the house I owned
for a while in Ranchitos de Galisteo. Dry summer,
hot afternoon.

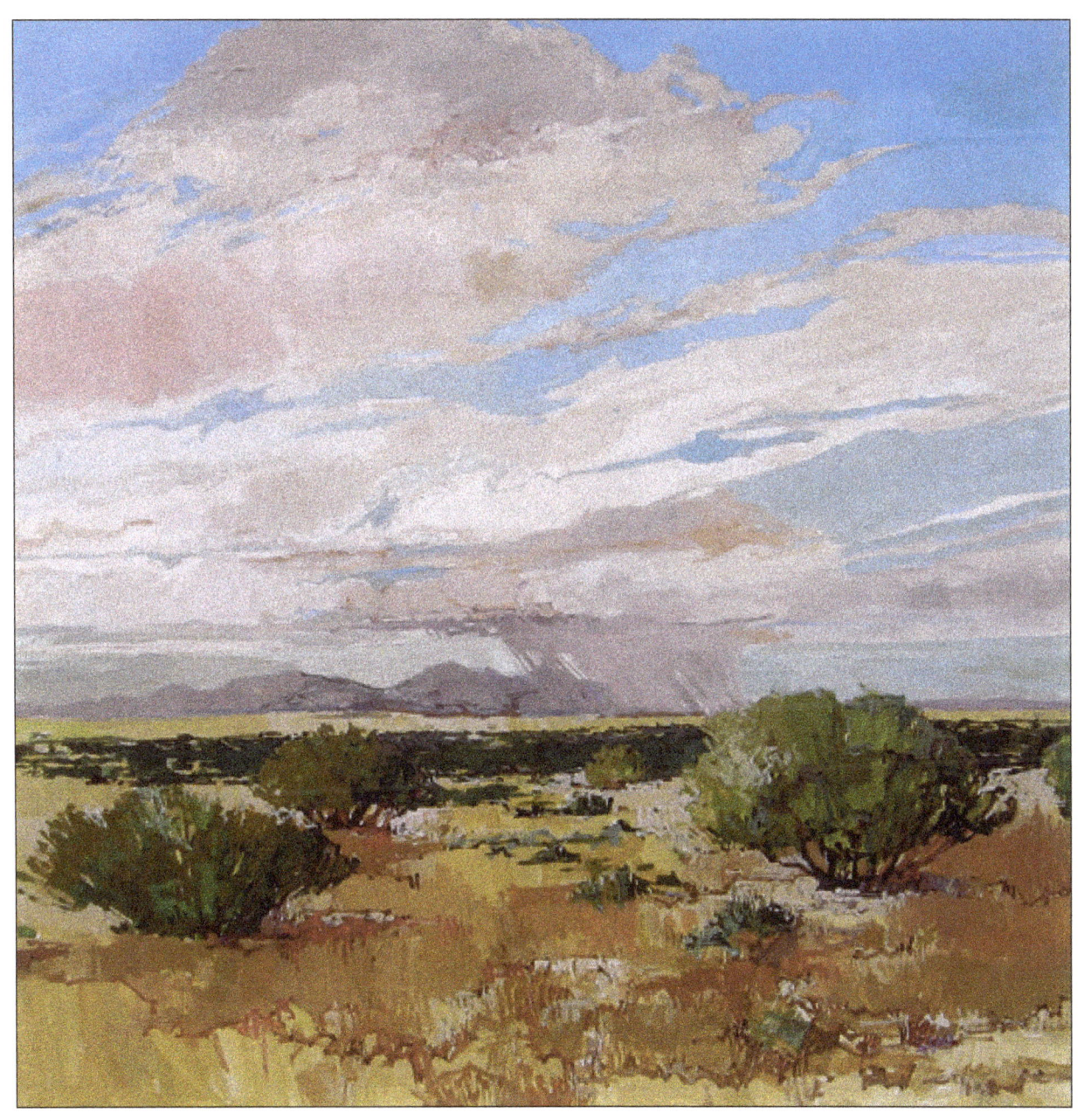

Mountain Church *18x18 Acrylic on linen canvas*

Another country church in the middle
of the New Mexican countryside. For me
there is a sense here of civilization not quite gone
back into the ground. Some group of people must
have restored the white stucco in the
not-too-distant past, still caring. The
wilderness here can be hard on the polite
surfaces of piety.

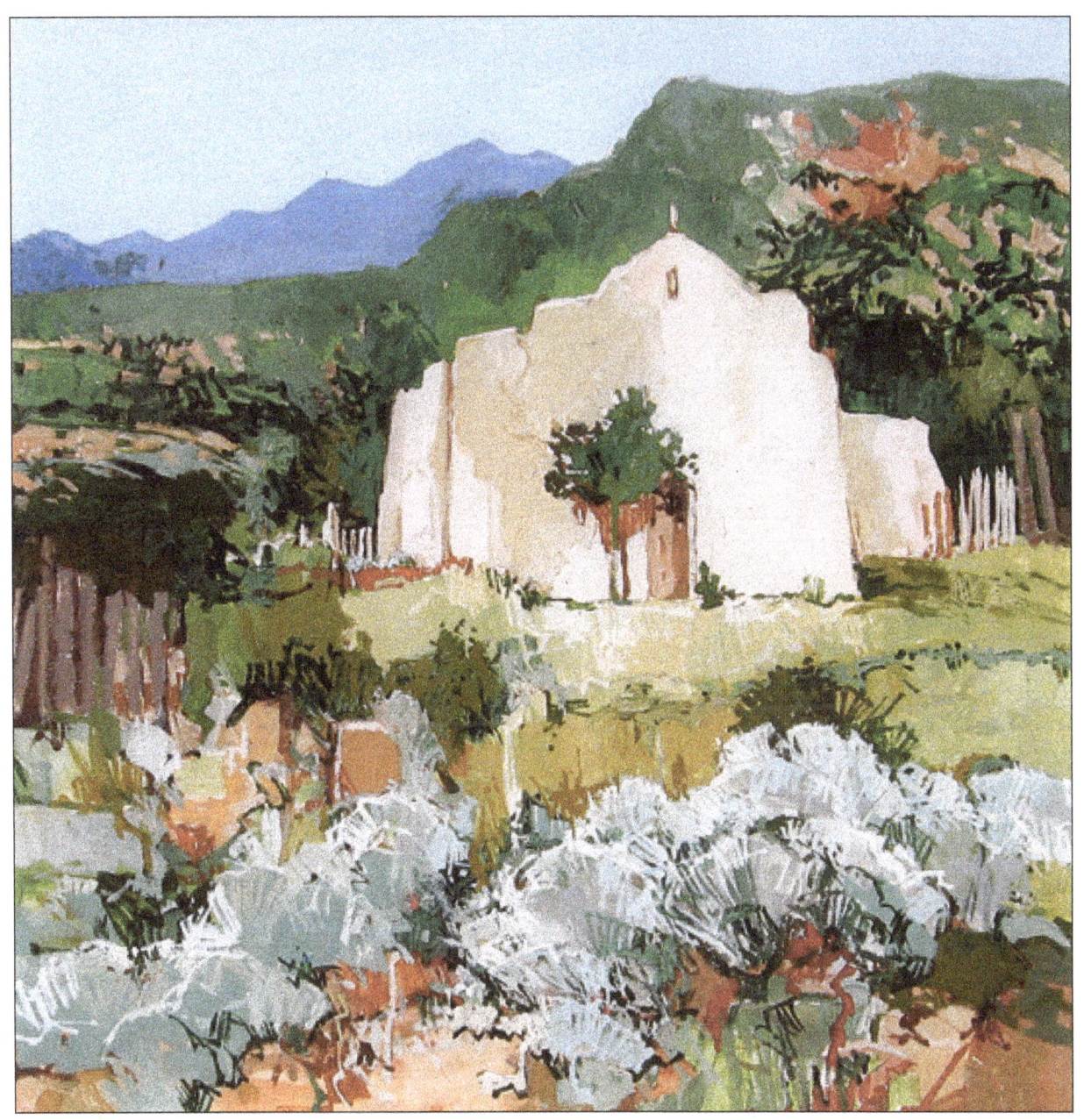

Black Canyon XI *24x24 Acrylic on linen canvas*

This painting gives some sense of the
stark contrast you see everywhere along
the Black Canyon rim. When not in the
full sunlight, the canyon walls recede quickly
into a warm black. When seen in the shade
of dark clouds, the walls almost hum.

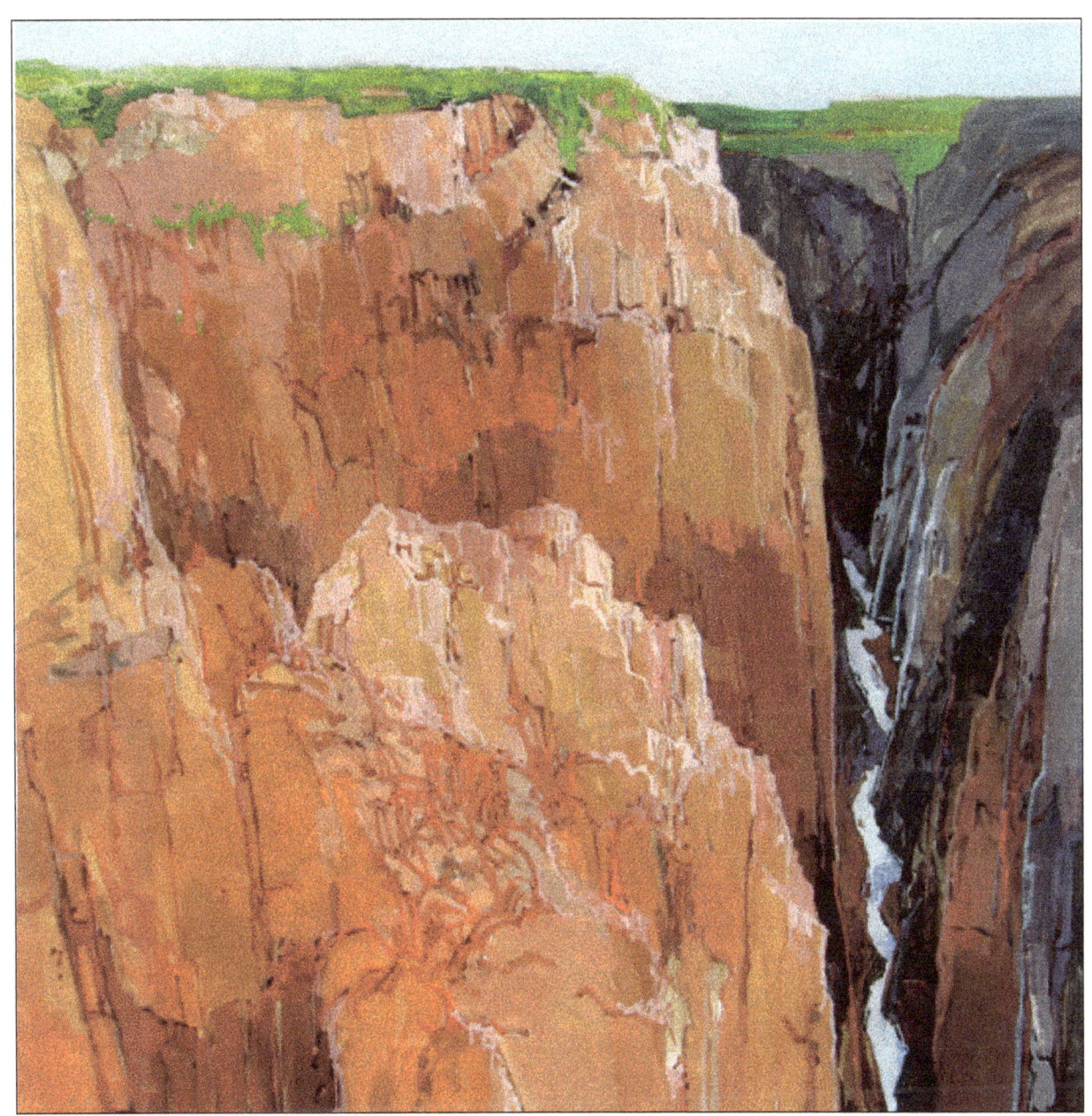

Black Canyon XV *14x14 Acrylic on linen canvas*

When in full light, the canyon takes on a
more friendly demeanor—blues, violets
and burnt siennas, very little of its namesake
black. This was painted from a
photograph taken by someone else that
I found on the internet.

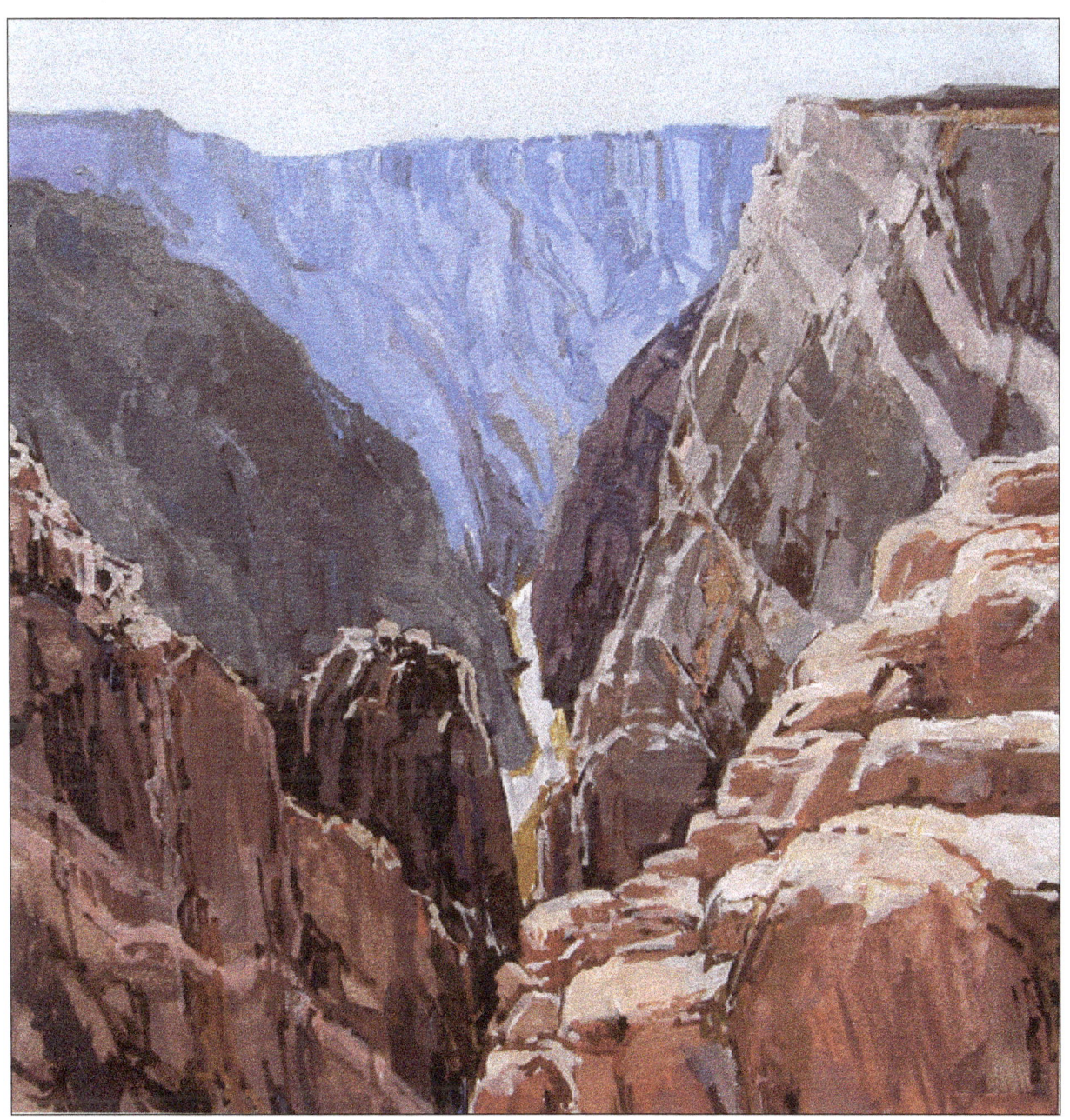

Bend in the River/Galisteo VIII *54x44 Acrylic on linen canvas*

This is a version of the motif that shows
the rivalry between red and green that is so
a part of the New Mexico landscape. In some
seasons of monsoonal rains, the green side wins only to give over
to the red side in a dry, late summer. The scene
is along the Galisteo River just west of Lamy,
a short walk from the road. I walked out there
recently and the pinons and junipers have
grown much larger, obscuring the handsome
red escarpment.

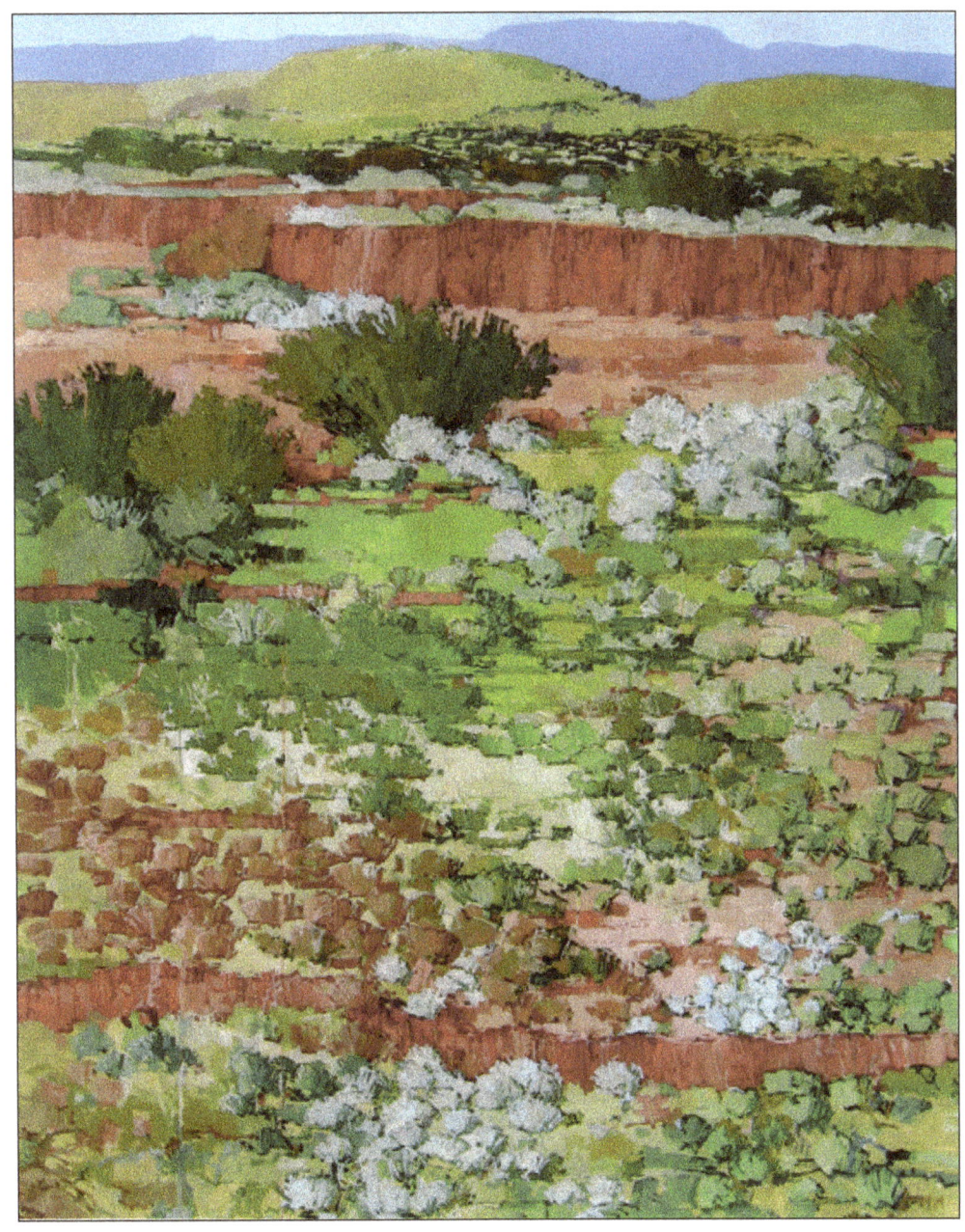

Galisteo

For as long as four or five years in the
1980s, Walter Cooper and I hiked around the
Galisteo valley every Sunday morning
before a late brunch at Souper Salad. Sometimes a
friend or two would join us, but usually it was only
the two of us. Skirting around rattlesnakes in the summer,
we found the remains of most of the abandoned pueblos, and
learned to recognize what constituted a suitable
site for a pueblo and the characteristic plant growth
over the fallen walls. But the crestons and their tapestries
of petroglyphs called us back again and again.
The next week I would report at cocktails to my friend
Agnes Sims, asking if she remembered
where certain distinctive ones were—the fabulous turkey,
the elegant long stalk of corn, the angry long-clawed bear, the warrior
with the shield or the two heads in conversation.
She always knew exactly where they were and often sketched
them out on a napkin. I never found a
way to use the rock art in my paintings, but
I painted the massive Galisteo crestons and escarpments
in many canvases.

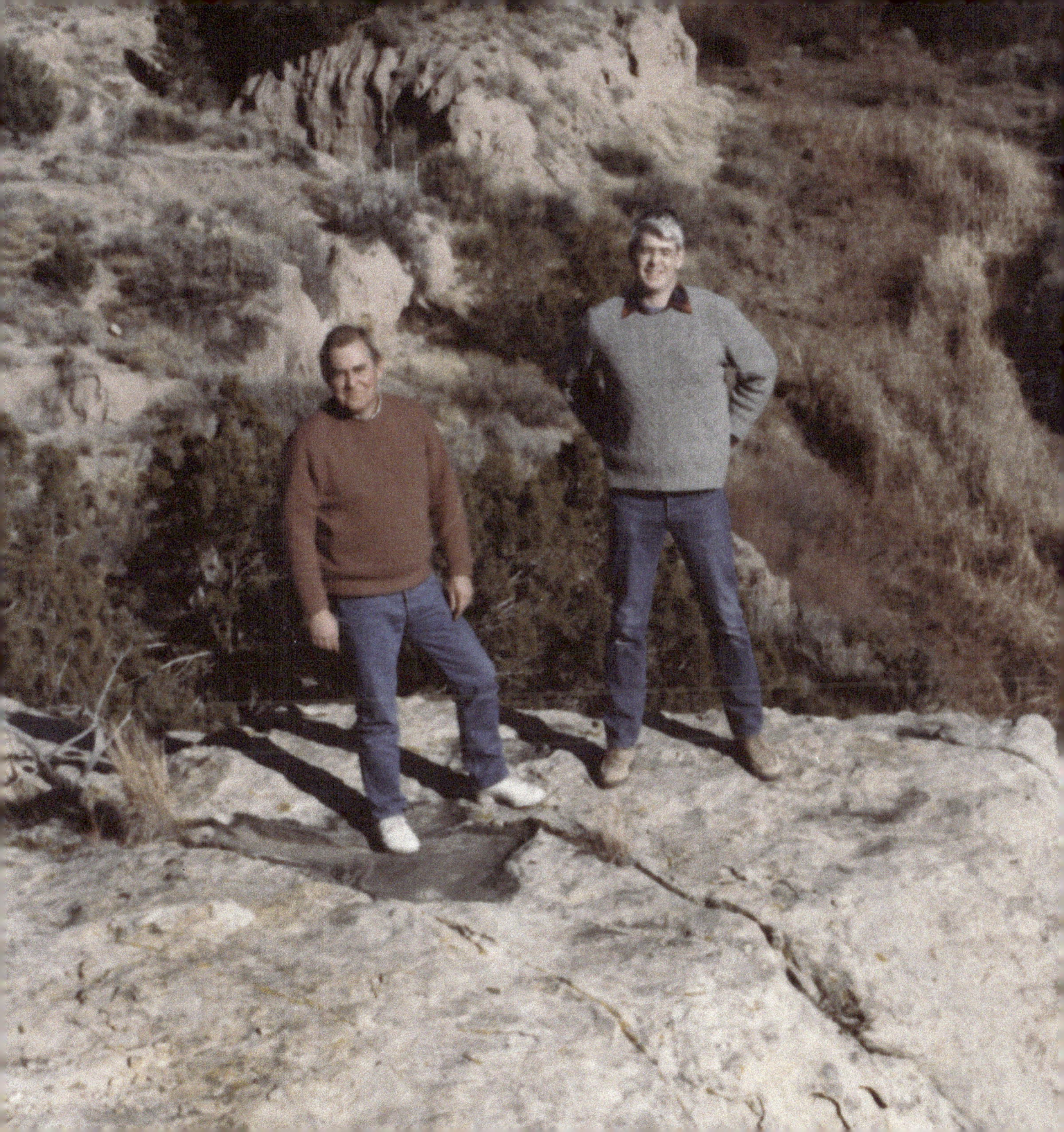

Running Man Mesa, Zuni *44x34 Acrylic on canvas*

If the Zuni are not especially lucky in other ways,
they are in having a seemingly endless variety
of cliffs, mesas, buttes, escarpments, volcanic plugs
and vistas off in every direction. The rhythm of the sienna red
and ochred white caught my eye in this scene.
Only after it was painted and framed did I
see the running man.

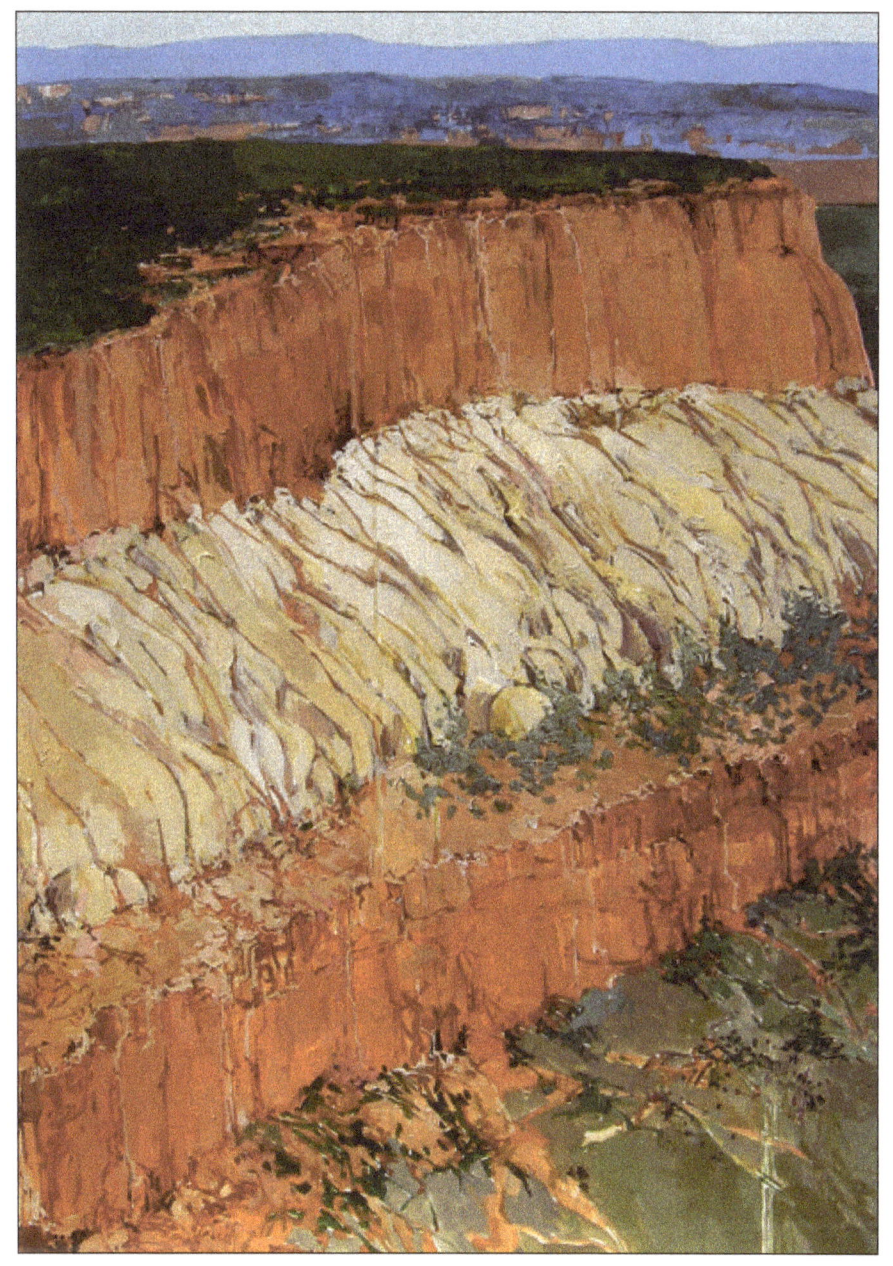

Galisteo — Britten's Bend *44x55 Acrylic on linen canvas*

This is a closer rendering of the bend in the river
motif. I had wanted to emphasize the horizontal
nature of things in Galisteo, how little of Matisse's
vertical plumb line is at home here. I was listening
to Benjamin Britten as I first put brush to canvas,
so it seemed right to give him a place here.

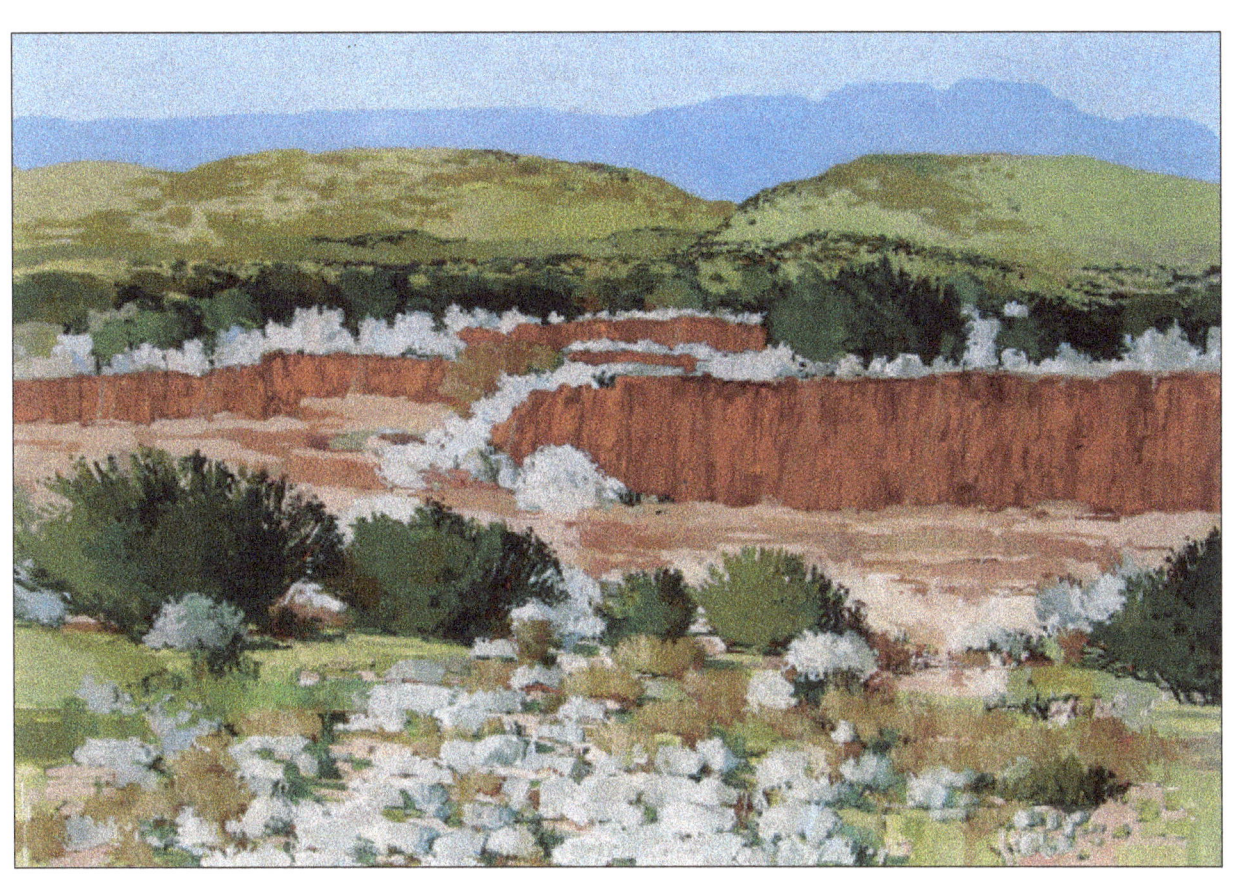

Rosemary's Garden *58x54 Acrylic on canvas*

A very proper herbaceous border, in the English
cottage style—a stone-edged demarcation between
lawn and border, clipped hedges as a backdrop.
This would be difficult to replicate in Santa Fe,
the hot sun here conspiring against so many different
plants in bloom at the same time.

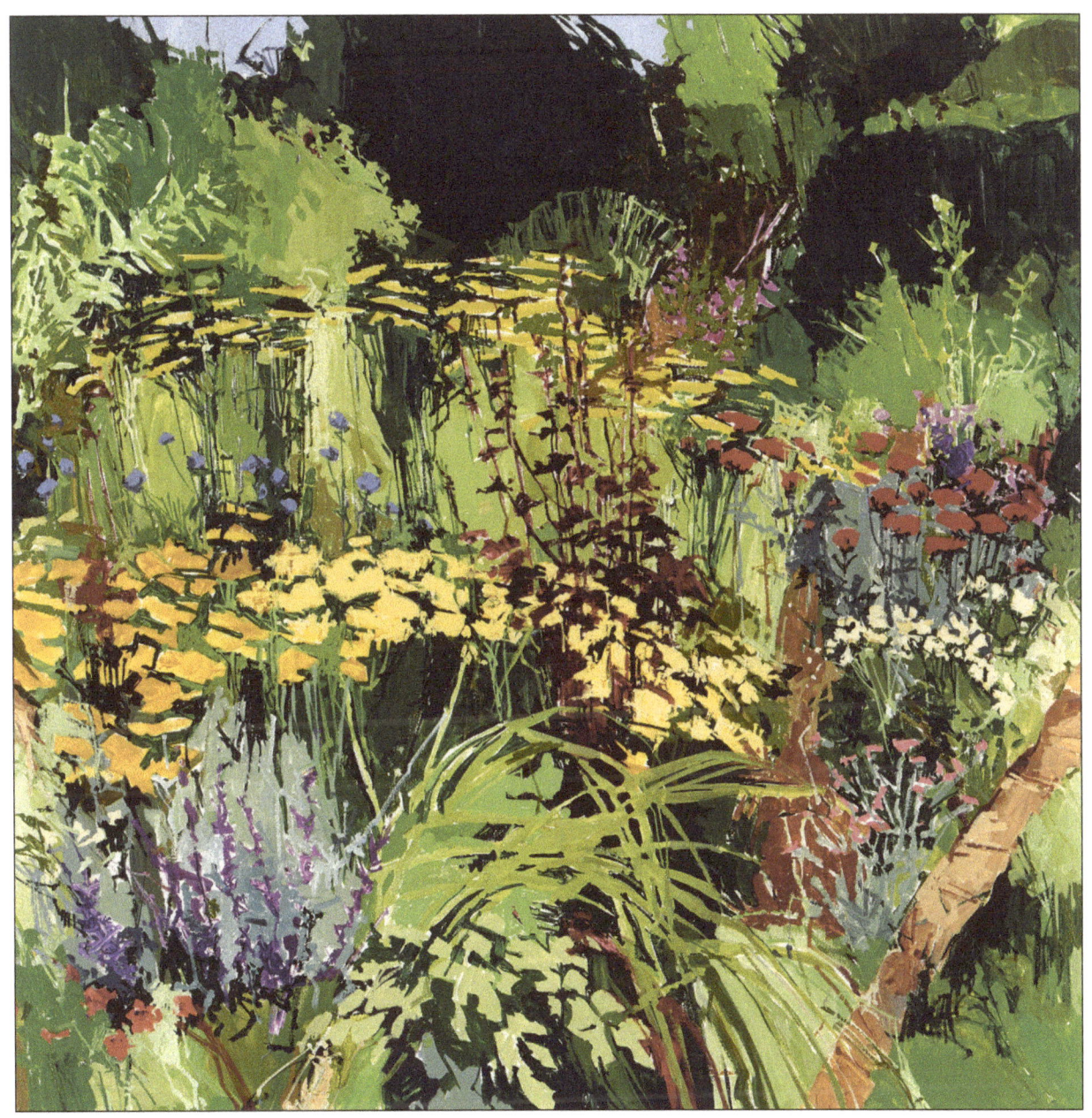

Nine Poppies and Yarrow I *48x72 Acrylic on linen*

This was a large canvas left over from another commission,
an extra I ordered in case I mussed up the first one.
I thought that the west garden along the entry drive
on Canyon Road could work well on this size.
It was a good project for
a long series of dark winter days, the yarrow
a cheery yellow where the sun was not.

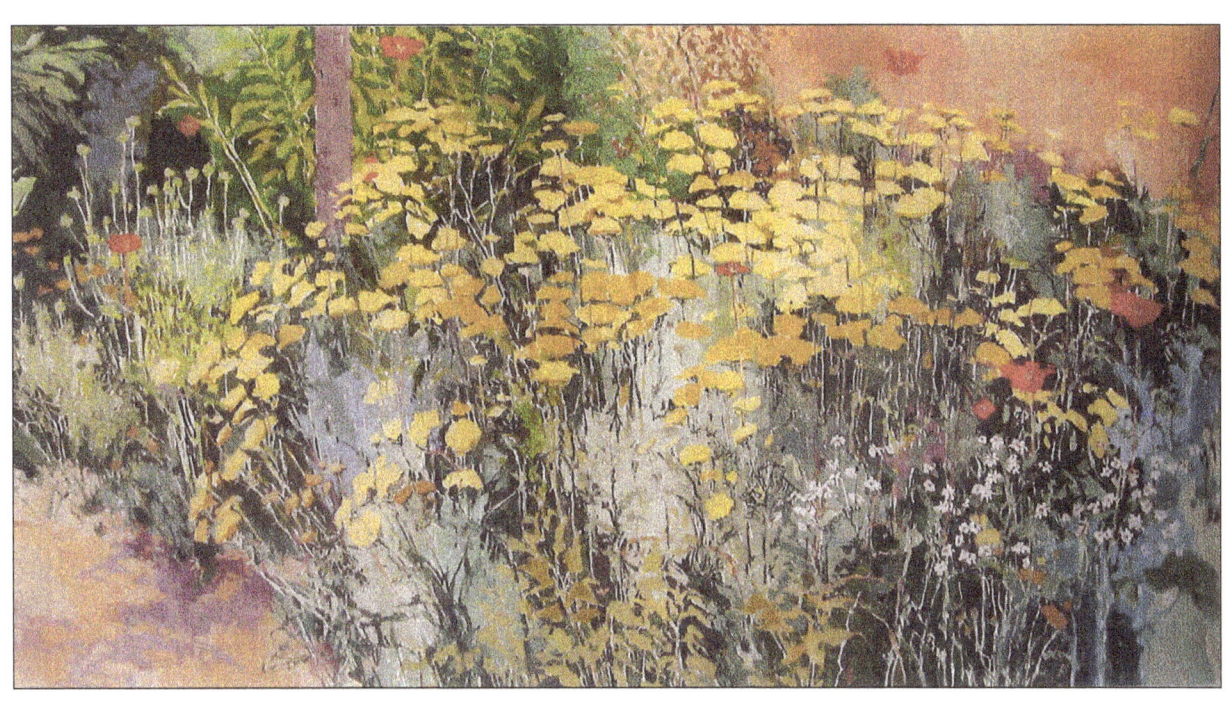

Summer Storm, Galisteo *44x34 Acrylic on canvas*

For a few weeks, late summer storms turn the grasses
in the basin into lush shades. Parts of the red earth
reflect up to the clouds in what could be
considered "artistic license."
In my book, any sort of summer clouds mean
abundance and plenty—even if
they are too reddish. Rain is
on the way.

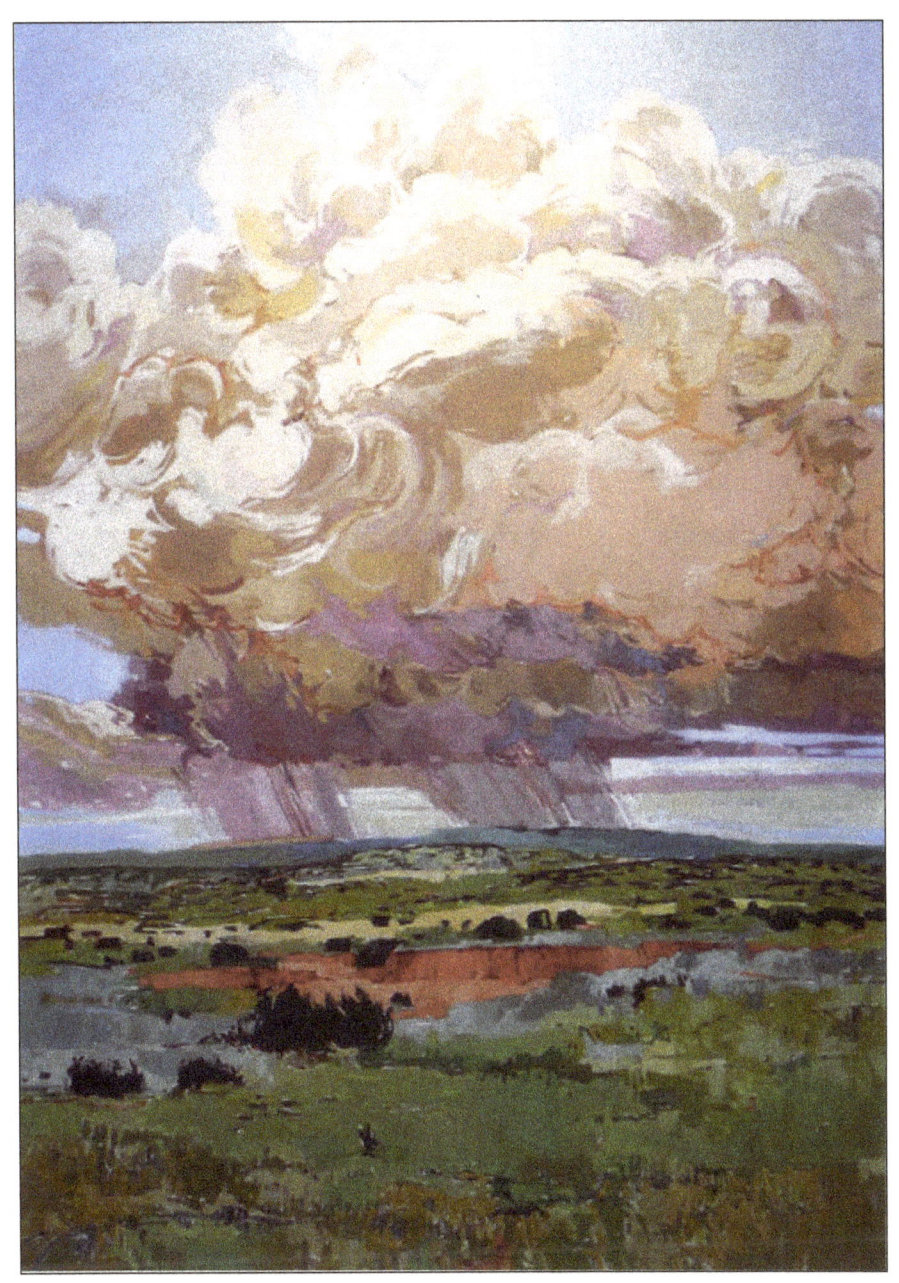

Garden with White Flowers, Commissioned *48x72 Acrylic on canvas*

The woman who commissioned me to paint this
wanted many, many white flowers with only the fewest of other
colors. It was fun to paint with so few general strictures
upon the design. When she saw the result, she had
trouble with the pathways in the corners, saying that was not
what she had in mind. In the end
she accepted it anyway. It is always a chance
taking on a commission, the collector seeing quite
a different image in his/her mind's eye, but it
is probably good for a painter to press himself
into accepting a commission. Just to
keep a foot in the real world.

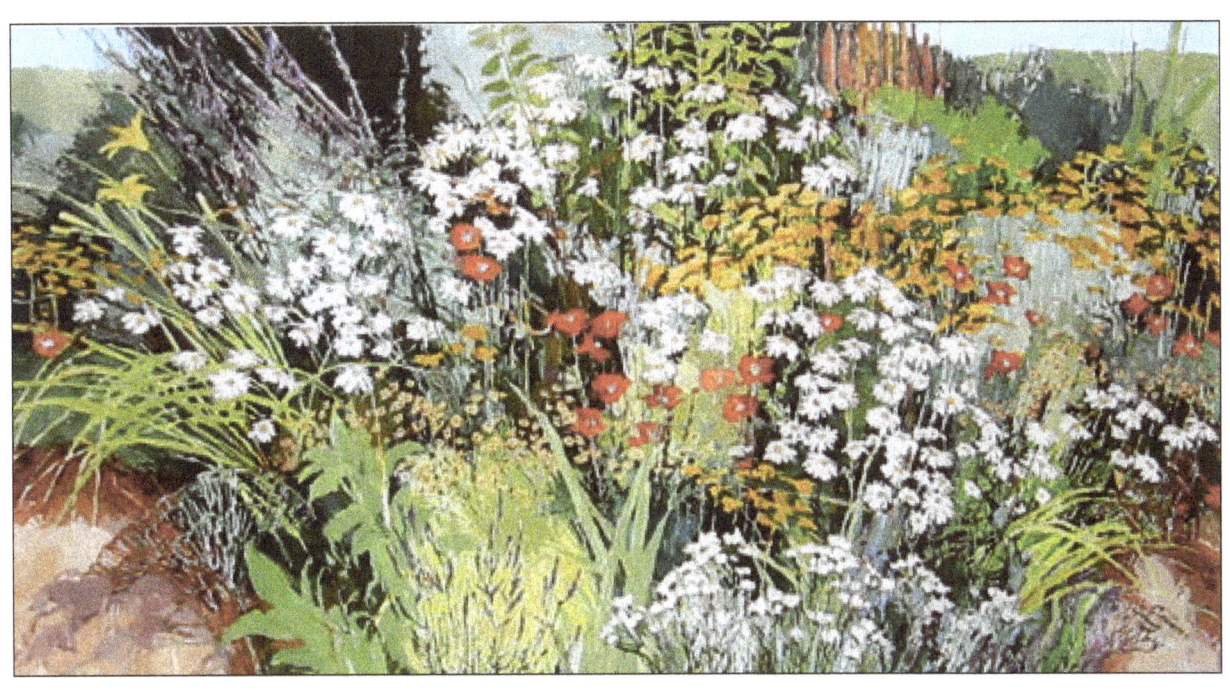

Front Garden Poppies *20x20 Acrylic on canvas*

I had always intended to plant more Oriental Poppies
in the front garden on Canyon Road. They are in bloom
only a few days and a fleeting subject, closing up by
mid-afternoon. I plan to have a separate area set aside for
them in my new garden on Cristobal Lane. Oriental
poppies do not play well with others,
and like peonies, should be planted in a long single row,
away from competition.

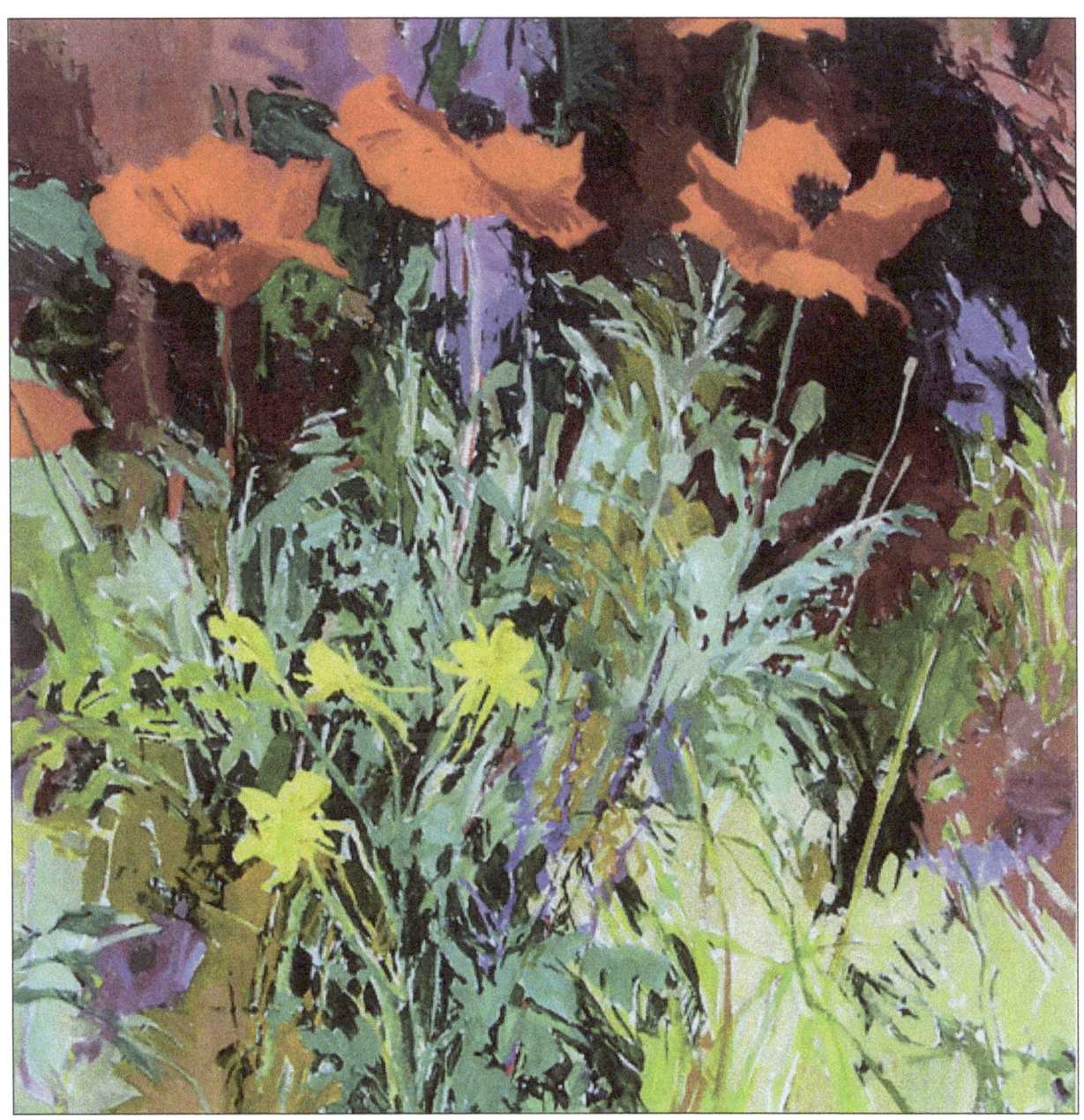

Twin Buttes at Zuni *Diptych of two 30x30 panels*

A summer scene of these iconic buttes, with a glimpse of the
unsullied land beyond. These paintings went well from the
outset, like days without clouds from sunrise
to sunset. A nice woman from Los Alamos came by the
studio while I was working and asked to buy
the diptych while it was still sitting on the easel.
Afterwards, I felt guilty about encouraging her to
do so, but two years later she told me that she
was still happy with her purchase.

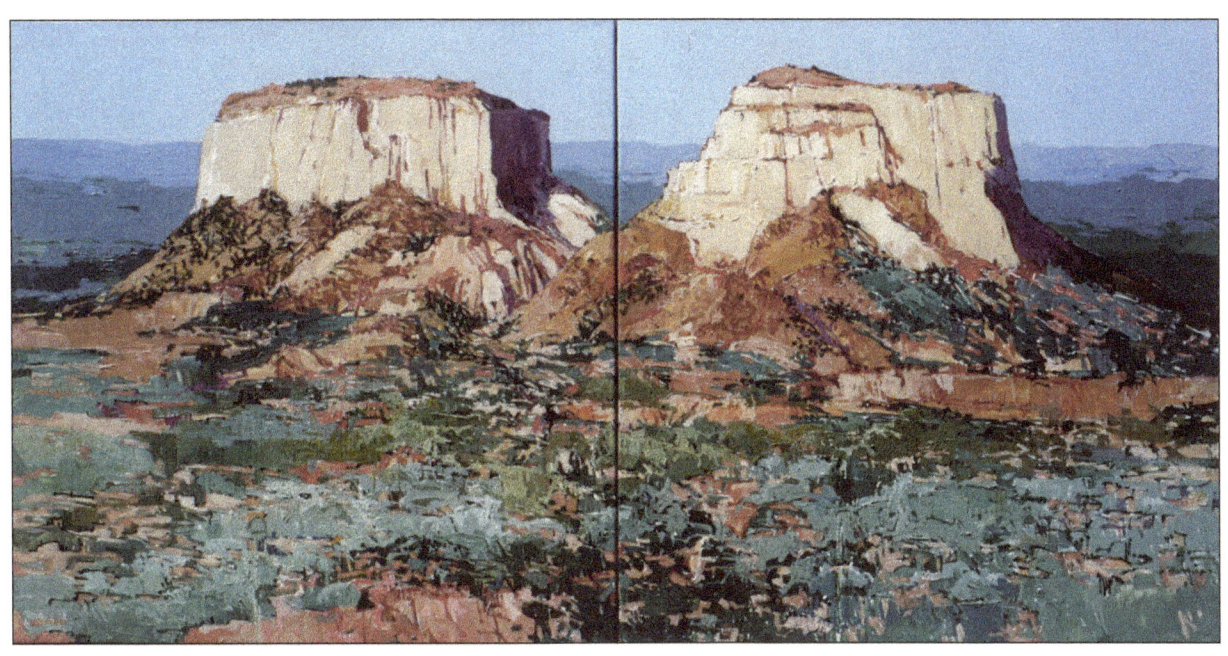

Garden at Penelope's *44x44 Acrylic on linen*

Another moist English garden, blooms fully open
in the soft, evanescent light. After my initial rush of envy settles down,
I try to pick up schemes that would work in my garden
in New Mexico. I come back from a trip to
the English countryside with the dictum that
you cannot ever plant too many poppies,
whether in Sussex or Santa Fe.

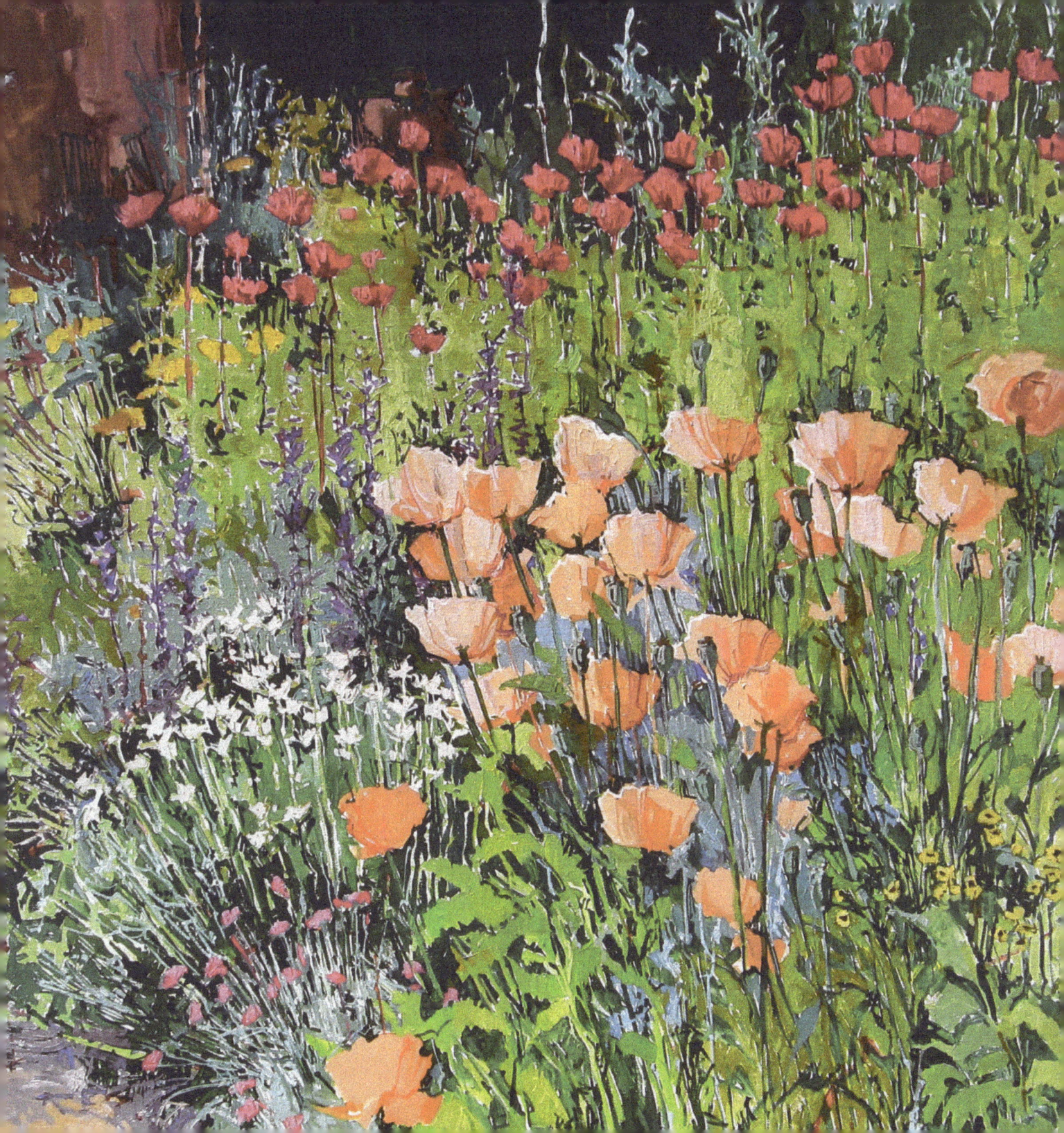

Double Cliffs At Galisteo *30x30 Acrylic on canvas*

For several years I drove out mornings to paint in the
studio I had built in Galisteo. I usually arrived early enough to hear
the couple who lived next door start their daily spirited argument,
the man slamming the door as he left while the woman continued her harangue.
His pickup scudded off in a cloud of dust. This view looking east is just north of the
village where the road dips down. I tried a few small
versions by the roadside, but this one
was painted in the cool of the studio. I can still
hear the couple arguing when I look at this.

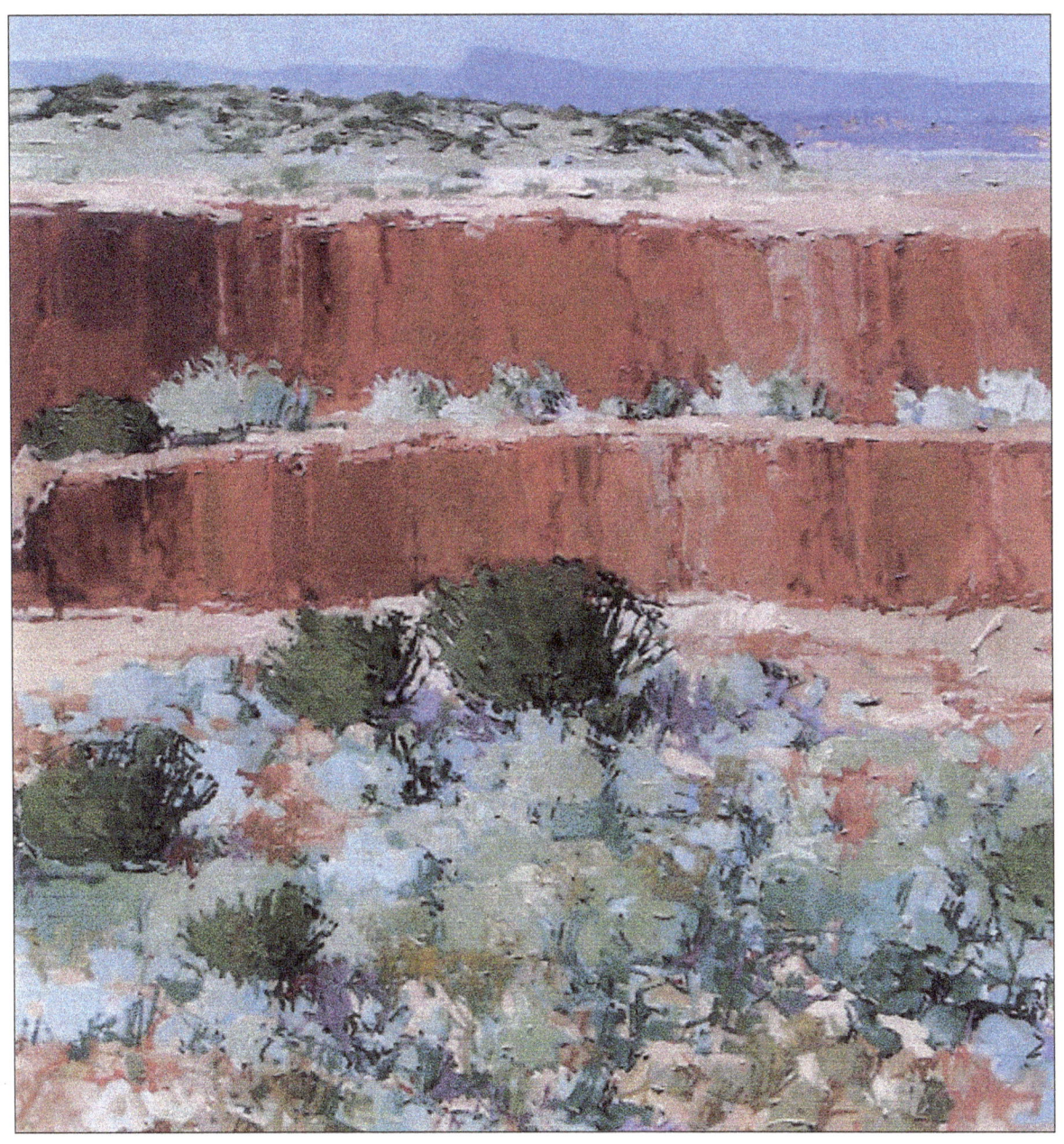

Kitchen Garden Poppies *24x24 Acrylic on canvas*

The motif without reference to
sky. Poppies tend to fall over after
a day or two in bloom, giving a nice
angle to the composition. This was from
a kitchen garden I planted on Canyon Road,
surrounded by a picket fence and apple espaliers.
I still think about the abundance of that
garden when I layout a new one.

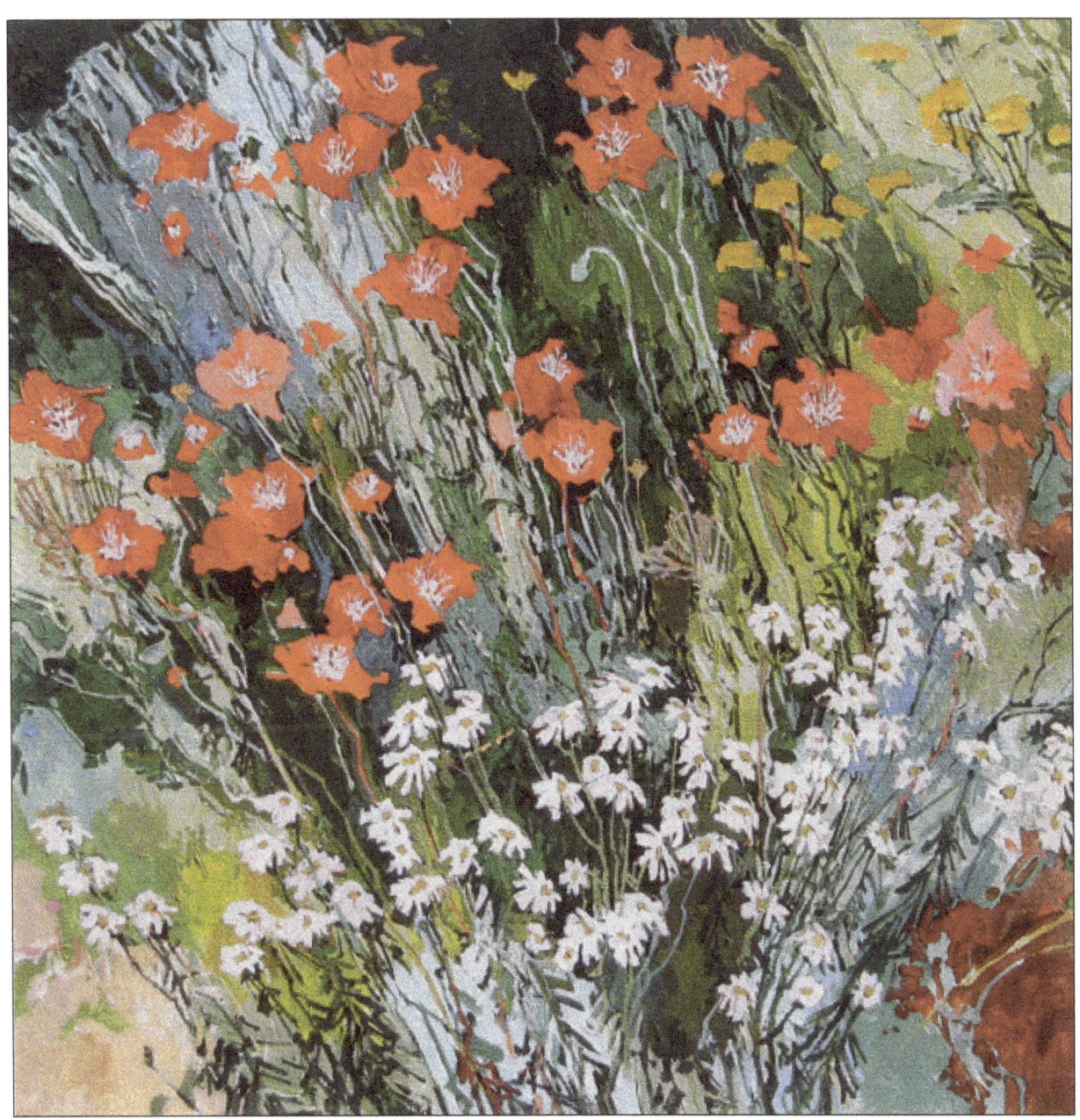

Sangre Hillside *18x18 Acrylic on linen*

This is a view from the middle of Santa Fe's
Eastside, where houses tend to crush in against
each other. I liked it that you could see only one
simple house in the foothills against
the mountains, as if it could have been the 1920s.
Or the way I imagine it was then, when nature
pushed gently against the cool houses where
reasonable people sat inside reading Thackeray.

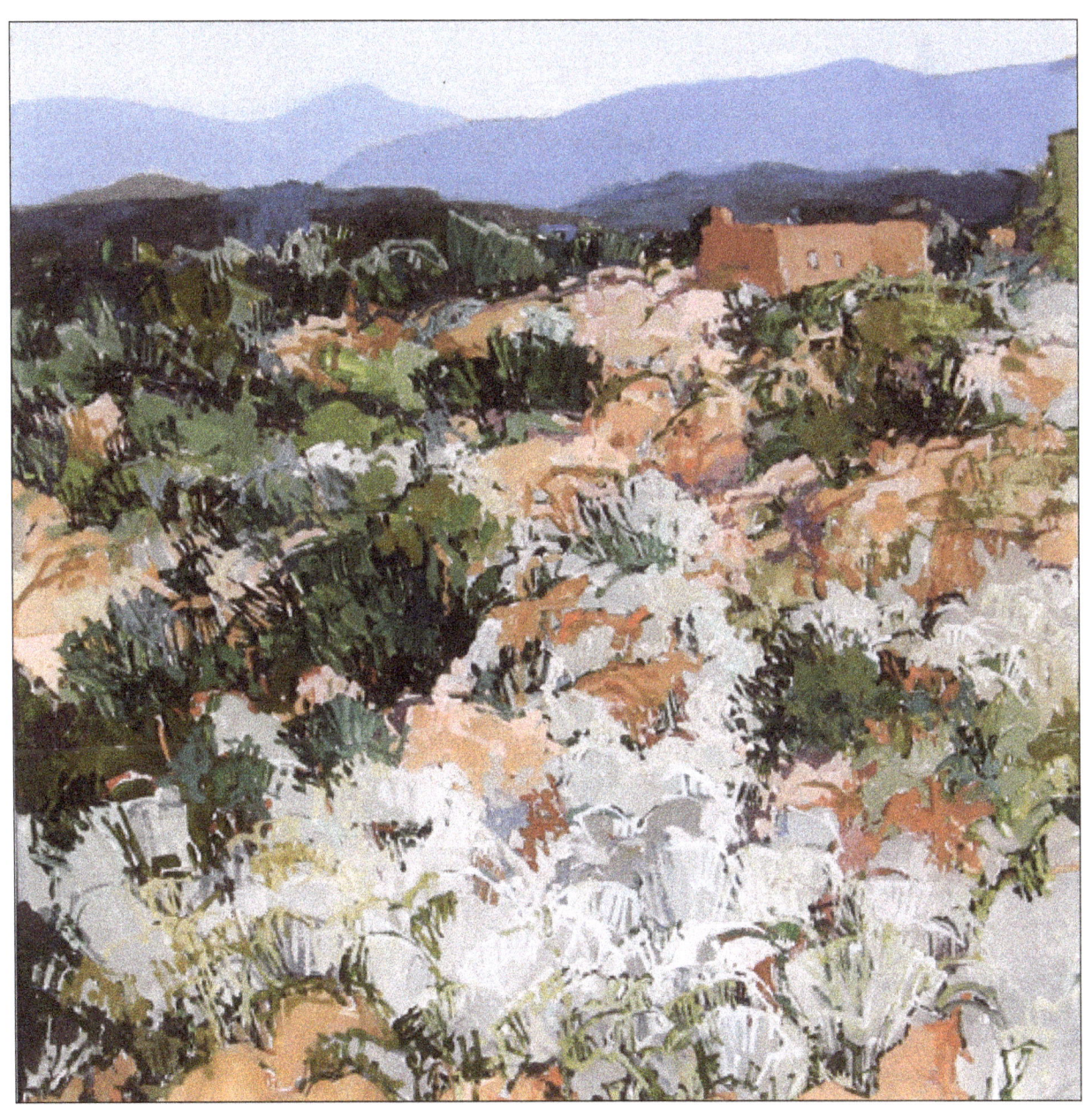

Zuni Cliffs *14x14 Acrylic on canvas*

Another of the splendid earth forms at Zuni.
This cliff parts in the middle to give a hint of
what lies beyond with a "V" for victory or
a sign of where no man has gone before.

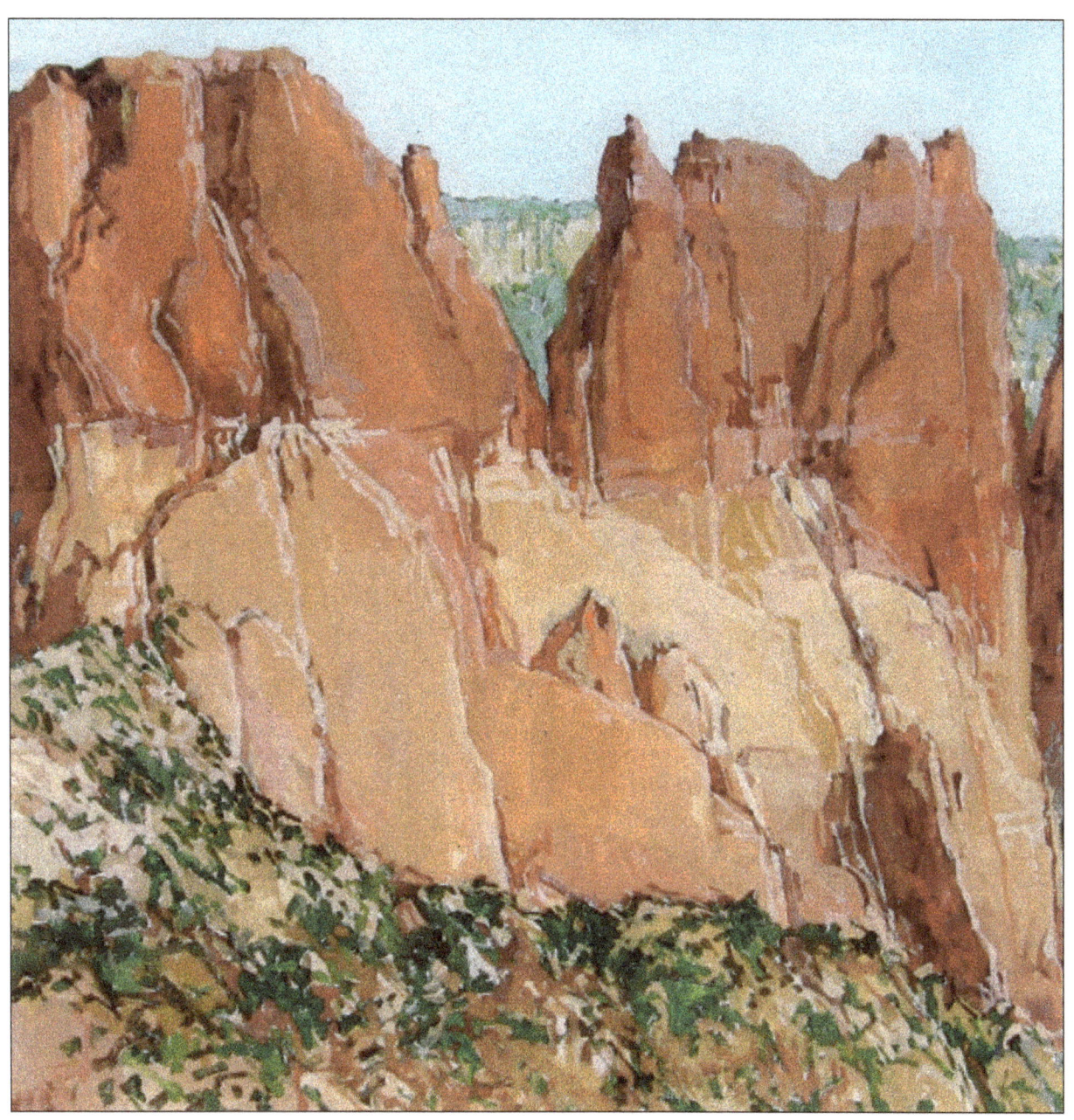

Hawaii Rainforest *58x54 Acrylic on canvas*

On a visit to my friend Ron Robles on Oahu, we walked
around in Honolulu's big Foster Garden
with mature tropical trees
and Heliconia varieties by the dozen. It was perfect
for sketching a dense scene like this as well as collecting
a full range of mosquito bites from the top of socks to the
bottom of shorts. In the Santa Fe studio,
later, a painting of this sketch was worked up. Robles
said that the greens were not quite right.

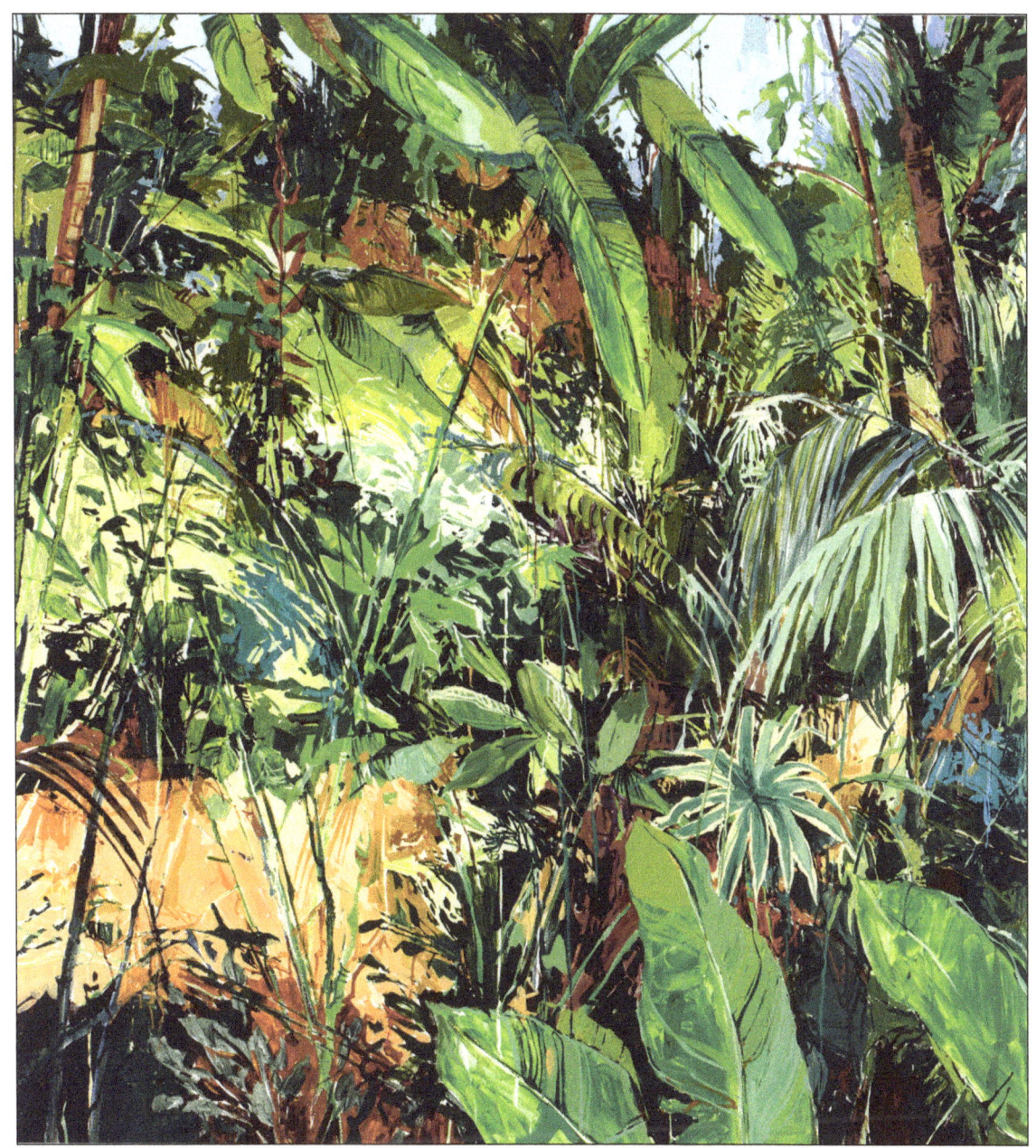

Heliconia, Barbados *12x12 Acrylic on canvas*

From the garden in Barbados, a glance
through the leaves at a heliconia blossom.
It seemed to have a certain Art Deco
quality to it, so I tried it on a
small canvas.

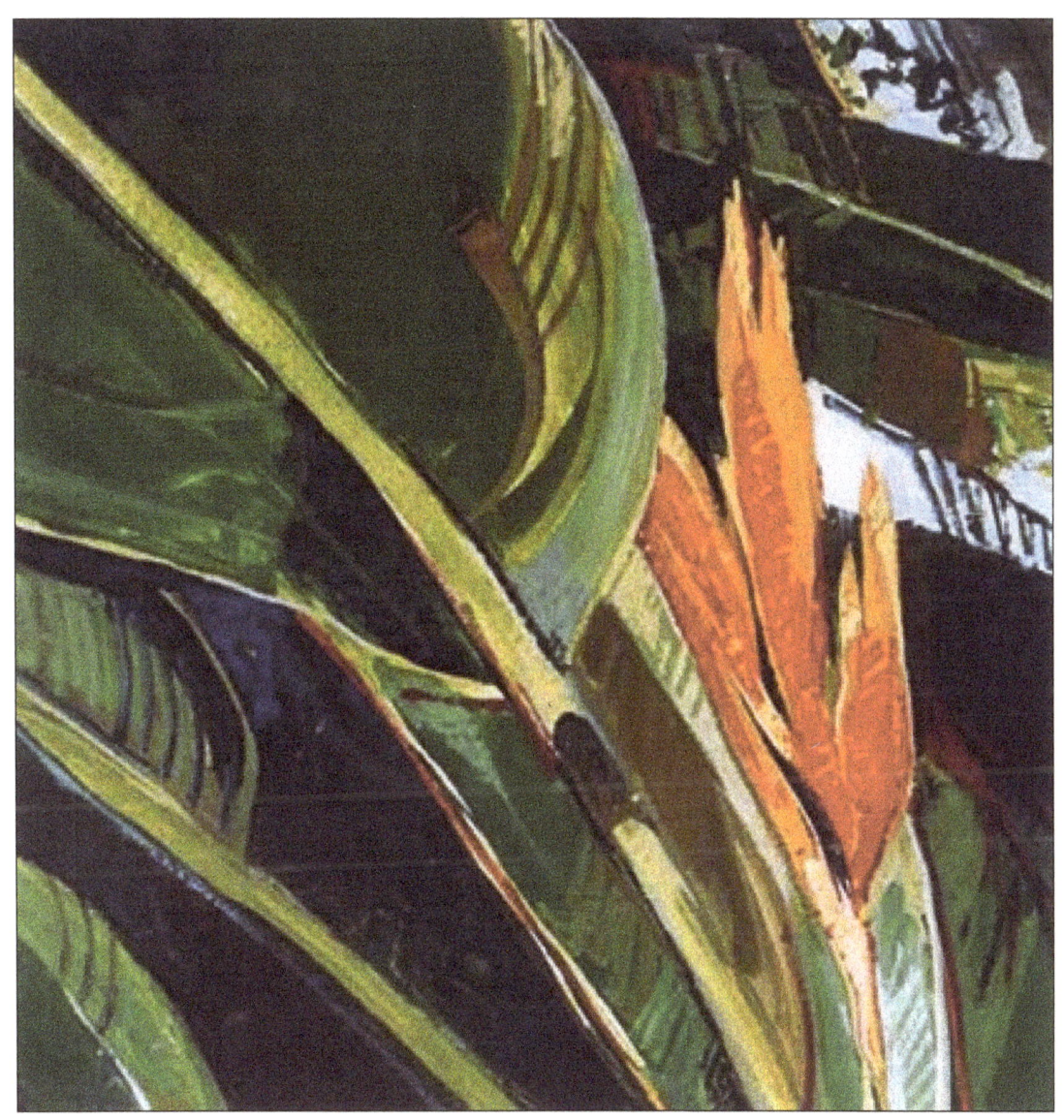

Studio Garden with Delphinium *28x28 Acrylic on linen*

Delphinium do very well in the cool nights of Santa Fe,
particularly in newer gardens where the necessary
trace elements have not been exhausted. They are tolerant
of the alkaline soils, as well. Competition
among serious local gardeners is keen to grow the
perfect stand of this perennial. This sky-blue version
bloomed well for several years in the Canyon Road studio
garden, creating envy among my peers. One "friend"
reported widely (just to stir the pot) that my
clumps of delphinium stood seven feet tall
with stalks as thick as broom-handles.

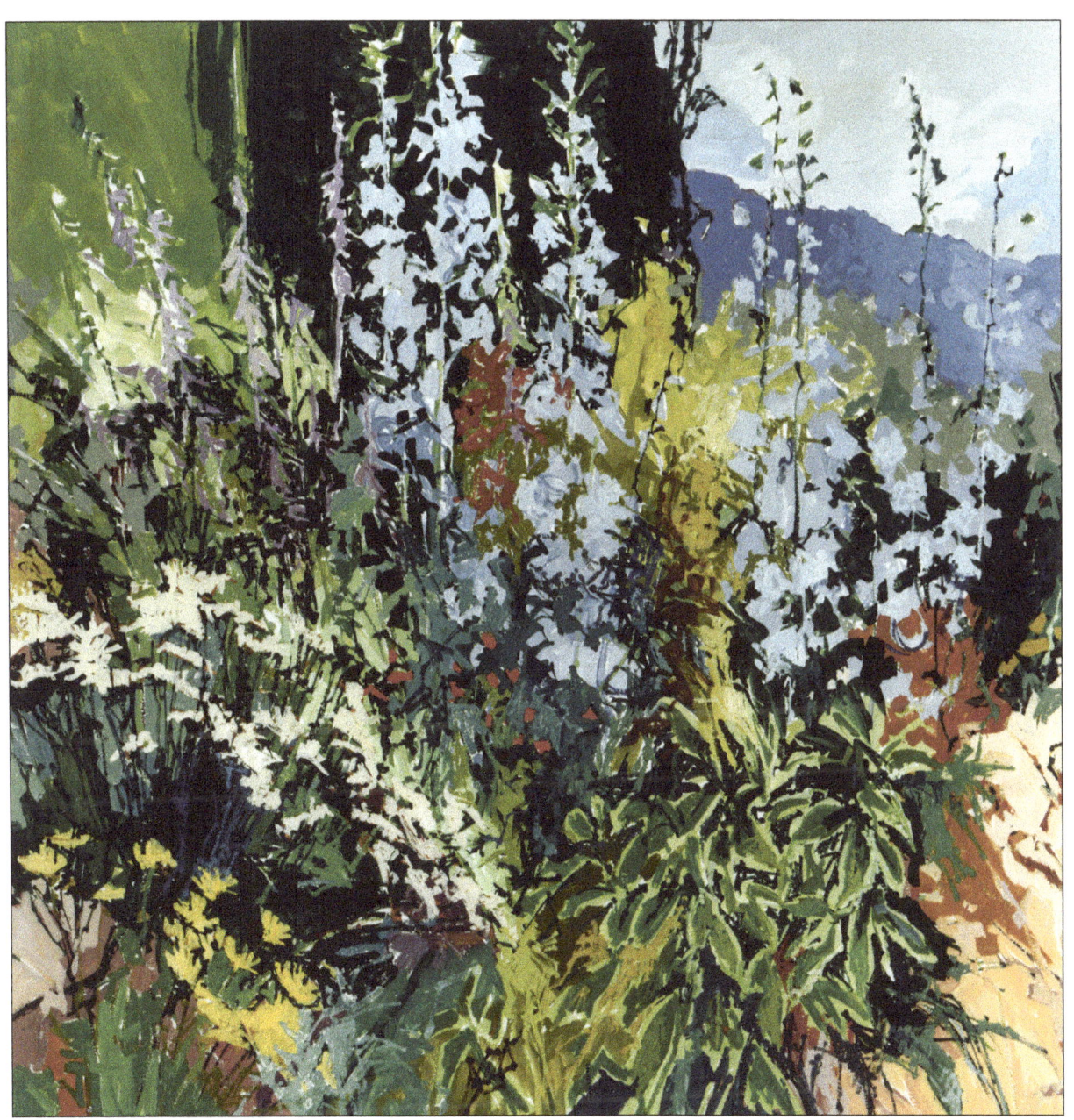

Aspens, Big Tesuque *36x36 Acrylic on canvas*

A small grove of aspens along the
Big Tesuque picnic grounds which year-in and year-out
offered an agreeable composition.
You do not have to hike very far for this one.
The raw sienna colors of the stream bottoms in
New Mexico are much more satisfying than
the dead gray and black ones of Colorado.

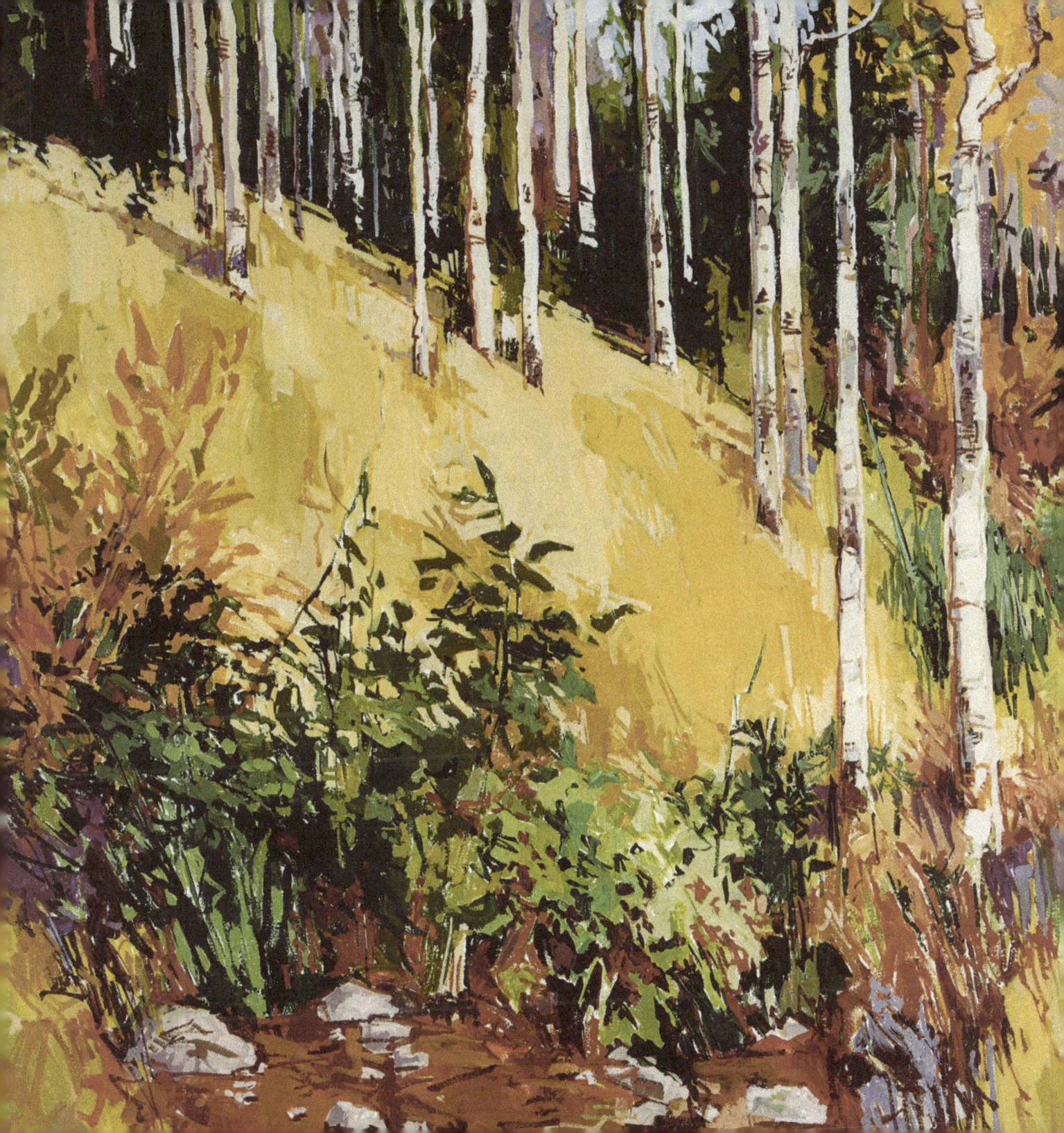

Escarpment Church *18x18 Acrylic on canvas*

Church against nature, again.
The innocence of the white against the
blasphemous red folds behind. Church
clearly winning here, but nature playing
her waiting game.

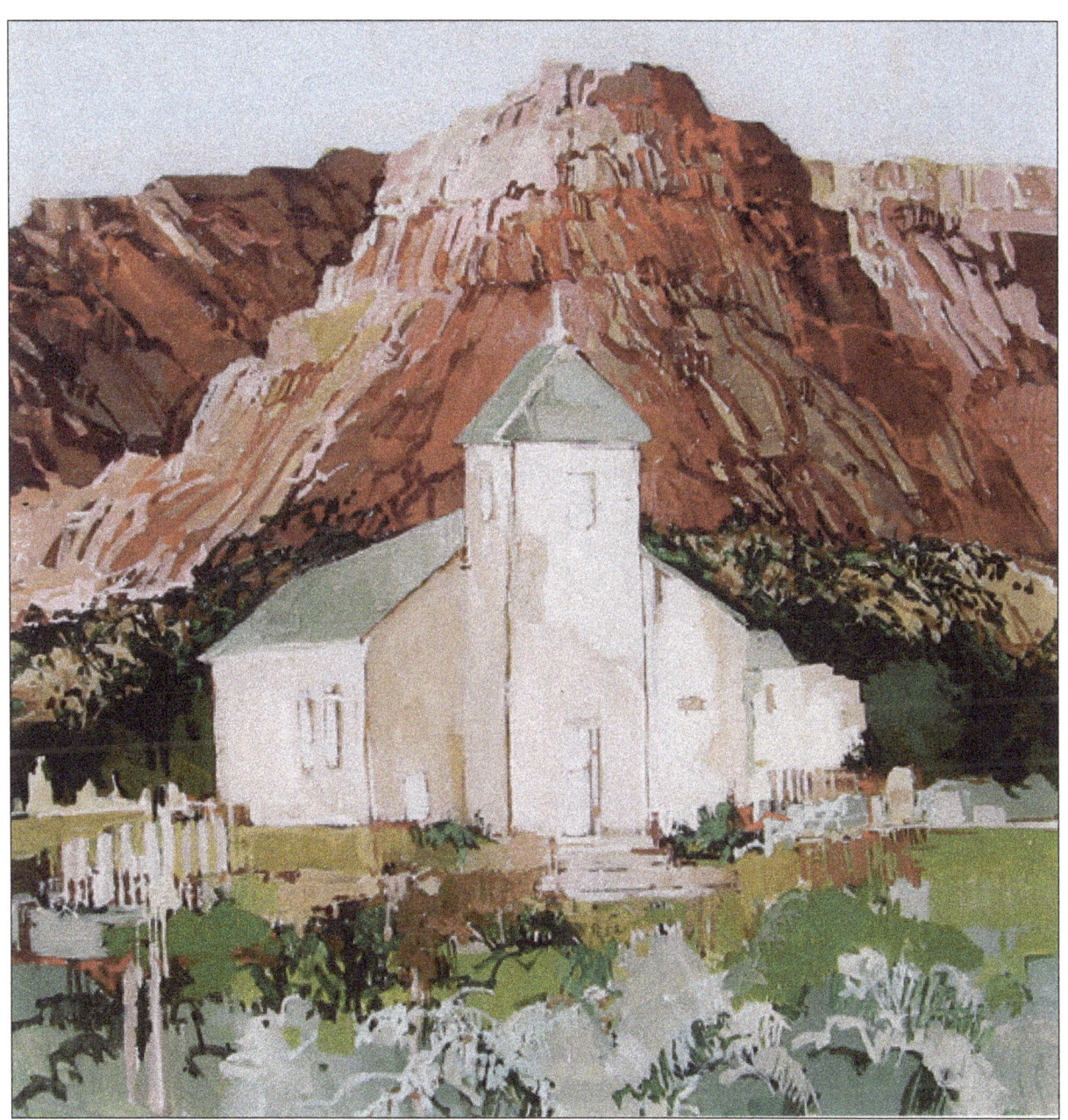

Abiquiu Mesa *32x32 Acrylic on linen*

This was the start of a series of landscapes with
a more designed, abstracted approach.
I wanted to leave some portions of the view
in a traditional technique, while morphing
to a graphic solution elsewhere. I also painted a
late afternoon version and a night one with
stars above.

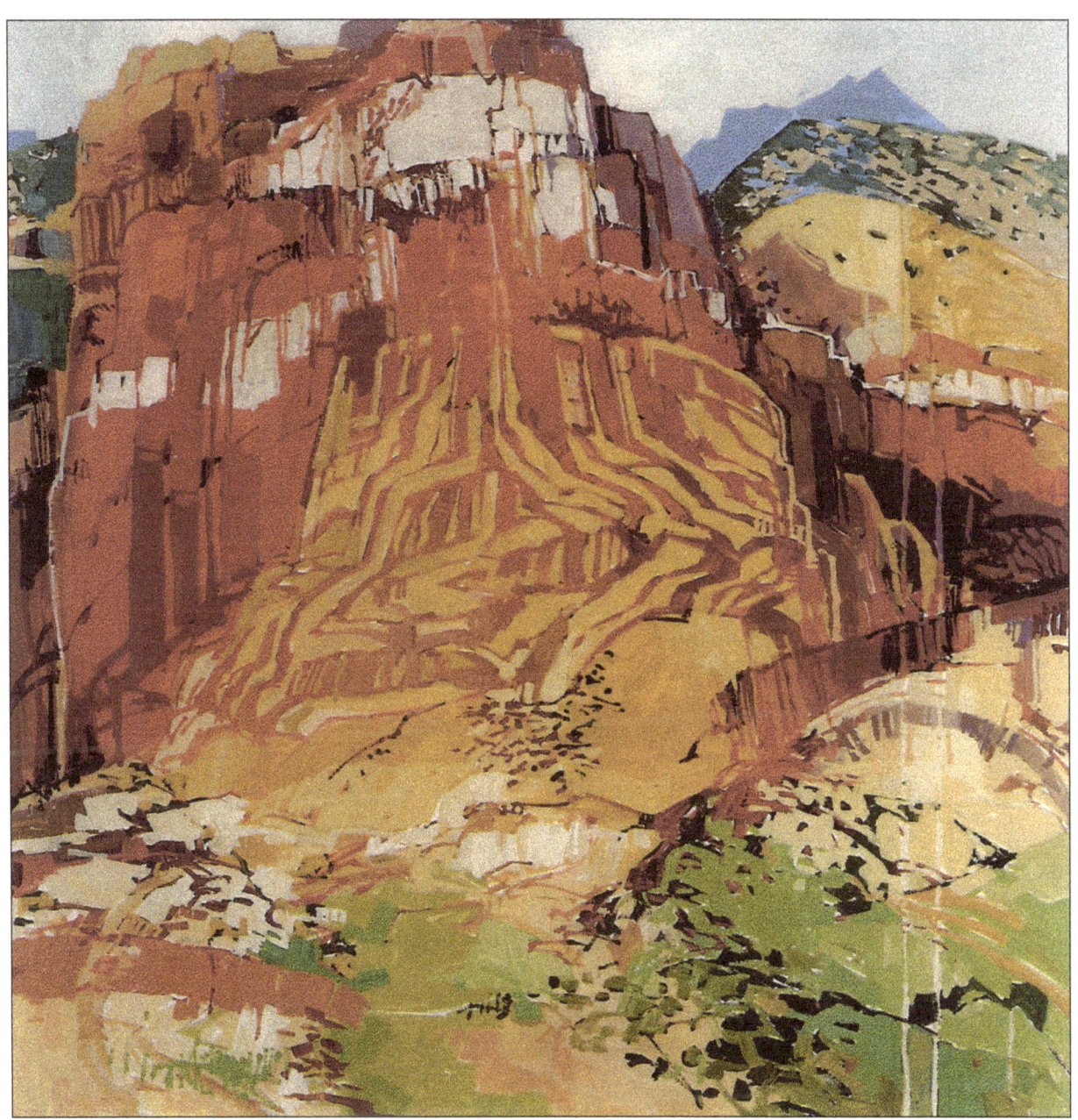

Westview on Comanche Gap *54x40 Acrylic on canvas*

A view from on top of the second dike when
Walter and I used to devote our Sunday mornings
hiking up there. The rocks look almost
quarried and brought up on donkeys, the ruins of
a building now heavily eroded. Sections of
Hadrian's Wall must have the same look.
The individual rocks are covered in
petroglyphs with solid-pecked designs
unique to this location. I hiked up here after
a snowstorm and found maidenhair ferns
still green and happy
against the warmth of the south-facing rocks.

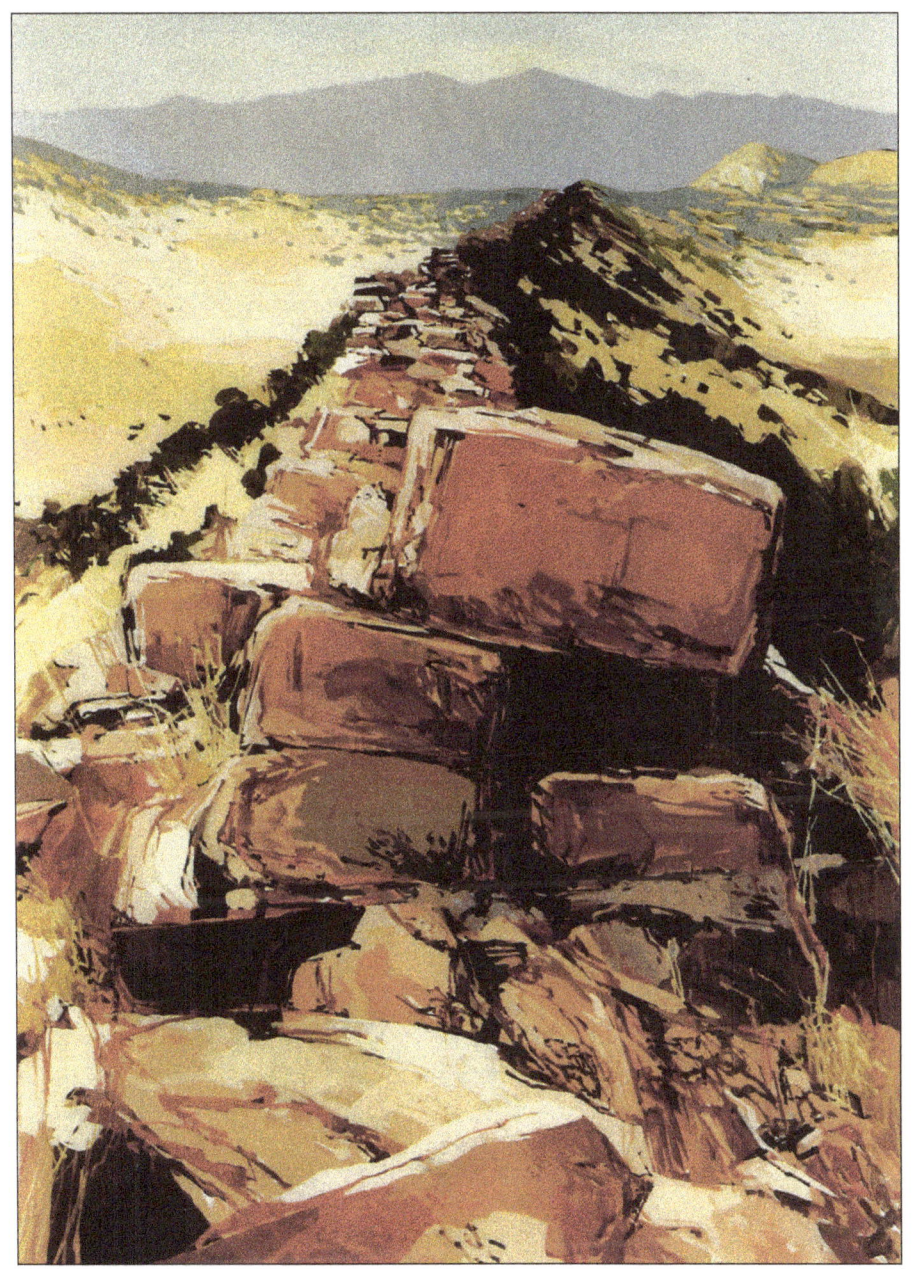

Lilies and Anthemis in Studio Garden *48x48 Acrylic on linen*

A scene from my Canyon Road studio garden
with orange lilies as the central flower.
I wanted to keep all the elements here in flat areas
of color, rather than bringing in highlights.
I purposely included a limited range of colors,
no reds or bright blues.

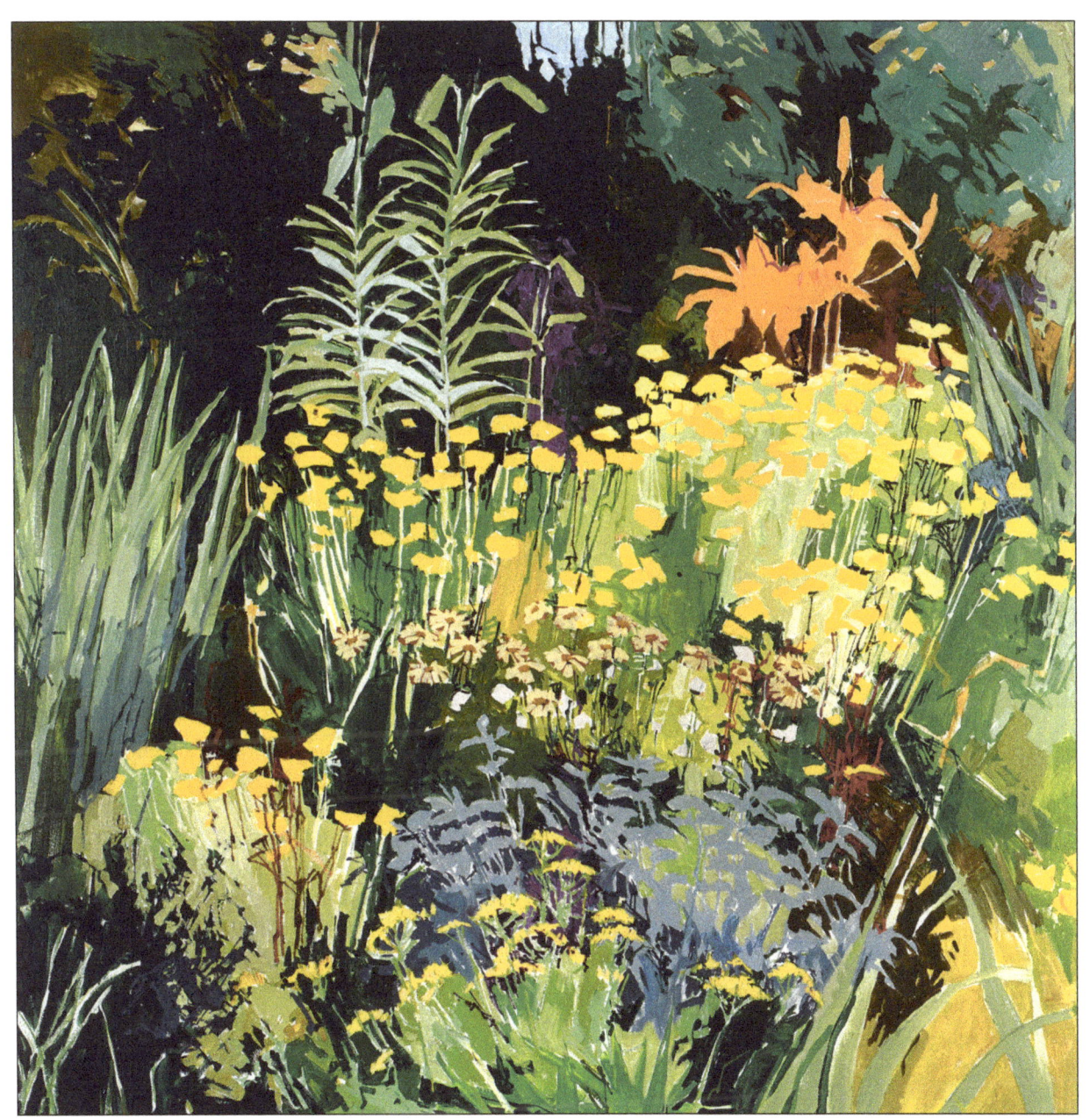

Westview South of Galisteo *58x54 Acrylic on canvas*

In dry summers the colors of the land
south of Galisteo village stay muted, pastel.
The dark green of the junipers gives a foil
to the pale array and the mountains almost
disappear in the heat. This is now in the
dining room collection at Quail Run.

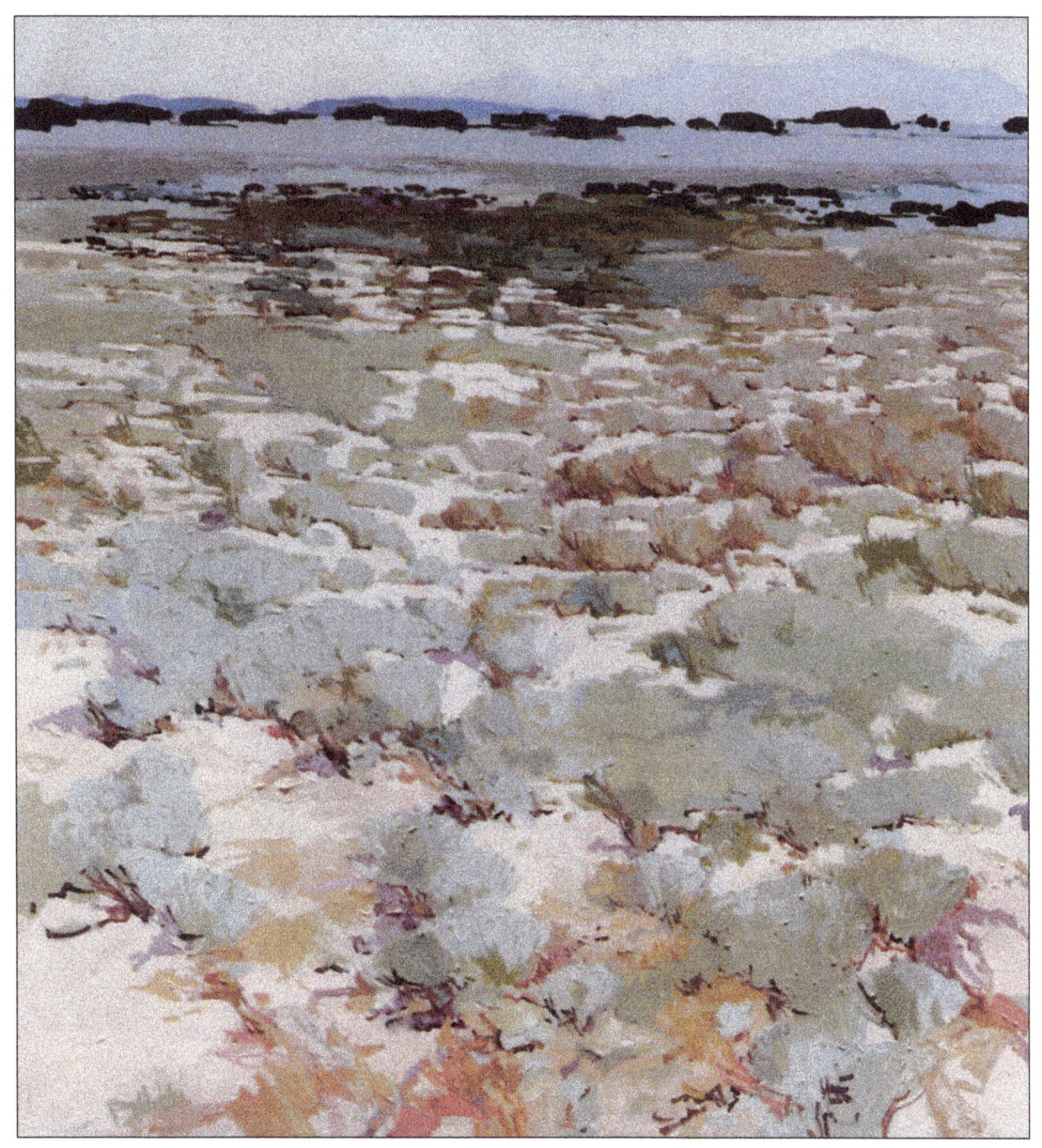

Galisteo Southview *16x16 Acrylic on canvas*

This small canvas was painted just outside the garden wall
of the house in Ranchitos de Galisteo on a windy
morning, looking across the red escarpments
along the river. A sketch, really.

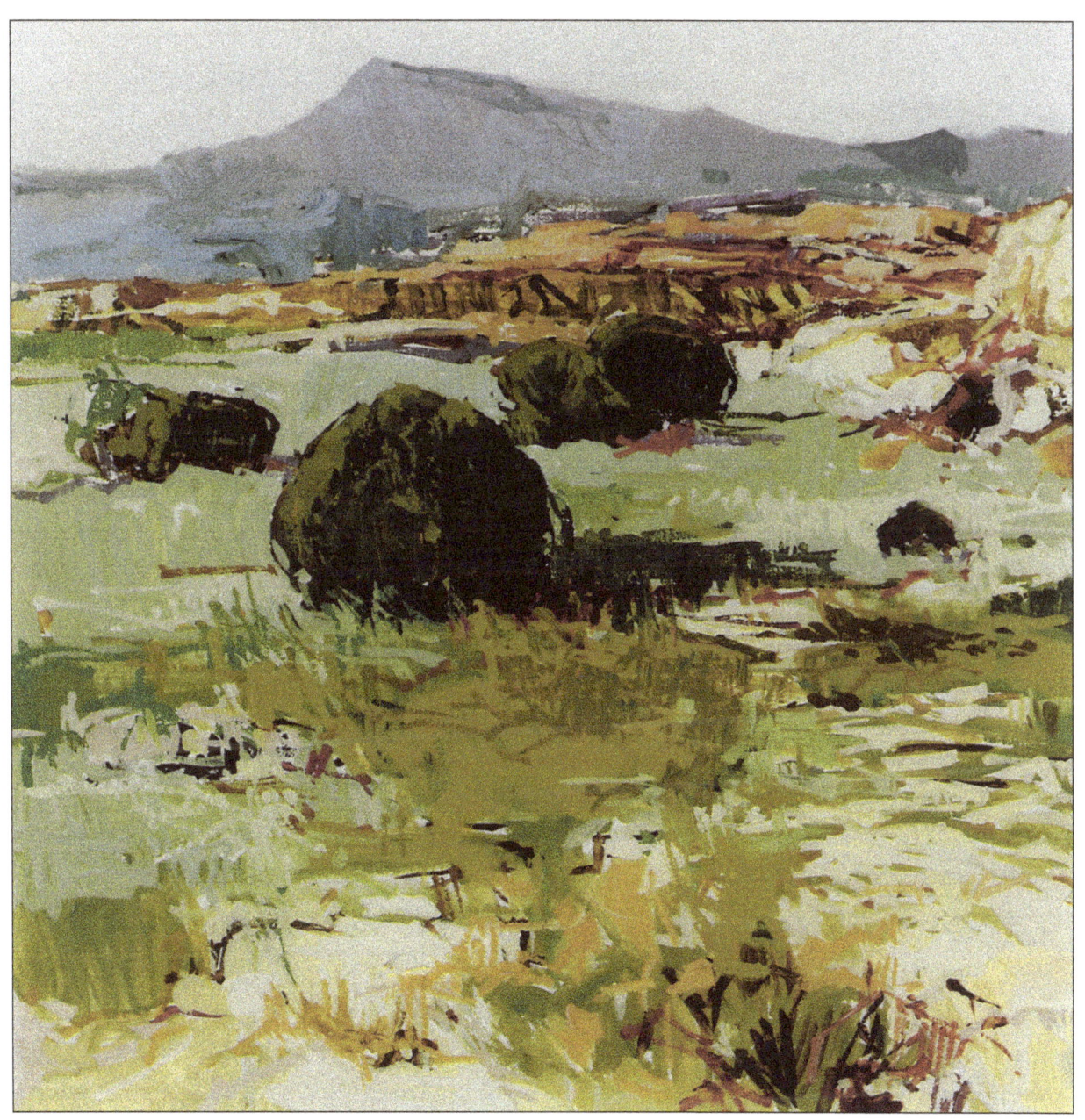

Siberian Iris with Garden Path *50x50 Acrylic on canvas*

I have completed several versions of this motif, and
if the garden wall blocks our view of the mountain,
the path beckons us on. The colors of
the flowers are in a very limited range, keeping
the scene cool but sunny. The odd large
leaf in the lower right serves to lead the
eye back into the middle of the composition. Despite
some tropical foliage, it is clearly a New
Mexico garden.

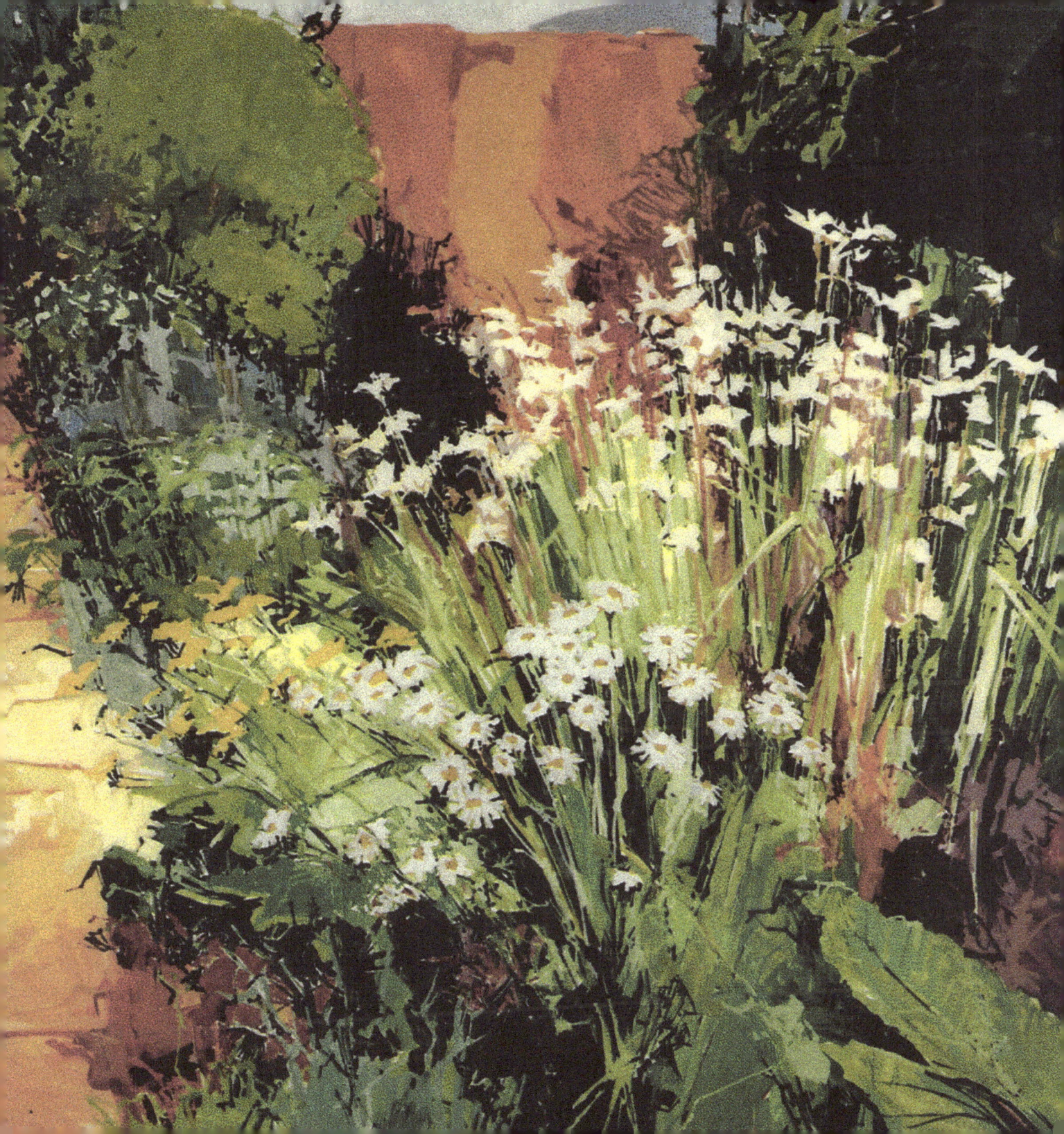

Late Winter, Big Tesuque *58x54 Acrylic on canvas*

This is a scene right after most of the snow
has melted in the mountains above Santa Fe.
The aspens are not yet in leaf and the grasses,
underbrush and small plants are still
in ochres and siennas. This was
painted from a sketch and several photographs taken
a short distance up from the picnic grounds.

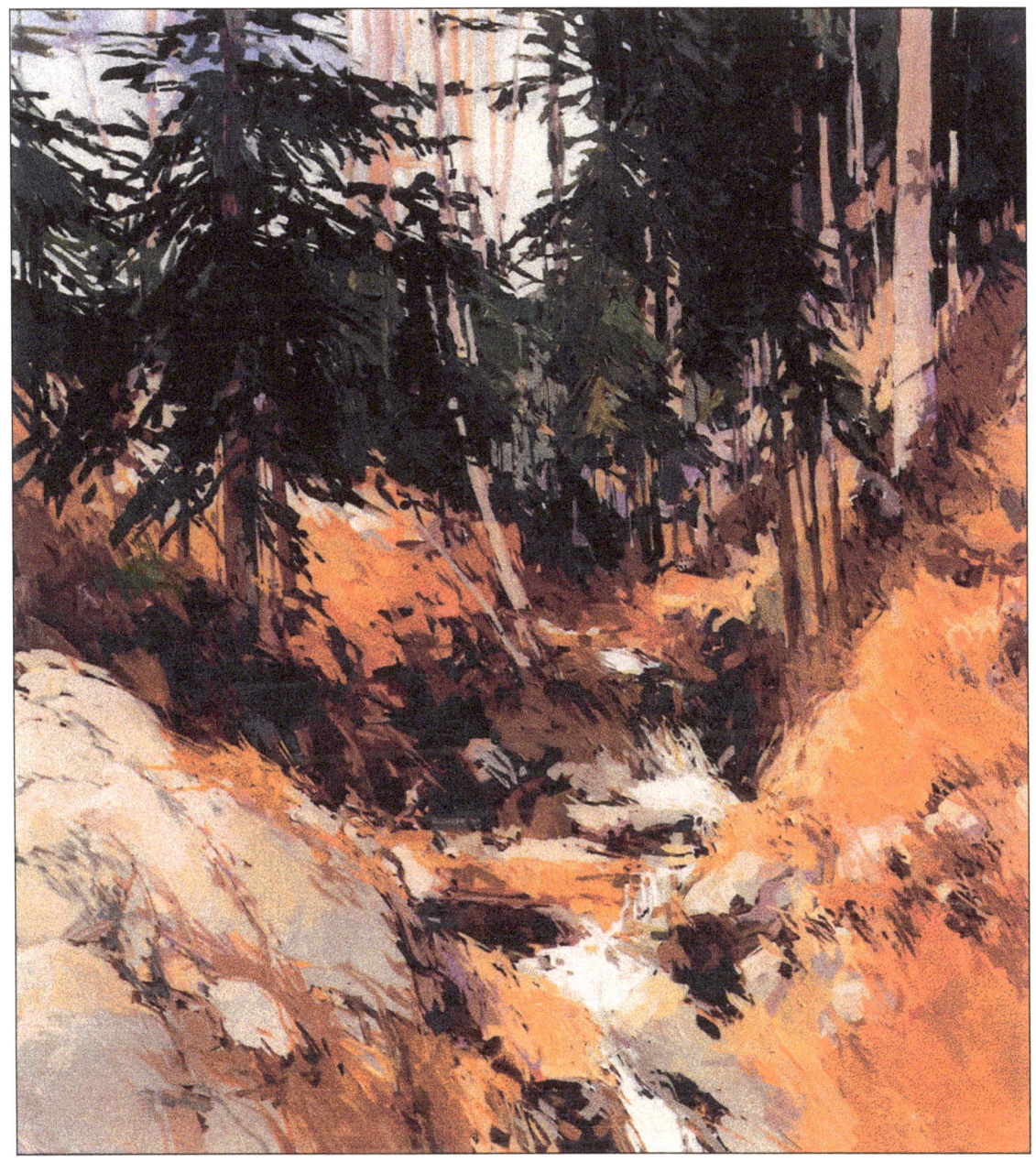

Tesuque Water Garden *44x44 Acrylic on canvas*

Some Tesuque friends Vernon and Buddy,
who were accomplished gardeners,
had a pond with all the traditional plants
of a water garden—water-lilies, iris and the like.
It was such an unlikely garden for New Mexico,
I enjoyed painting this one of a series.
I wonder if the pond still thrives under
the new owners.

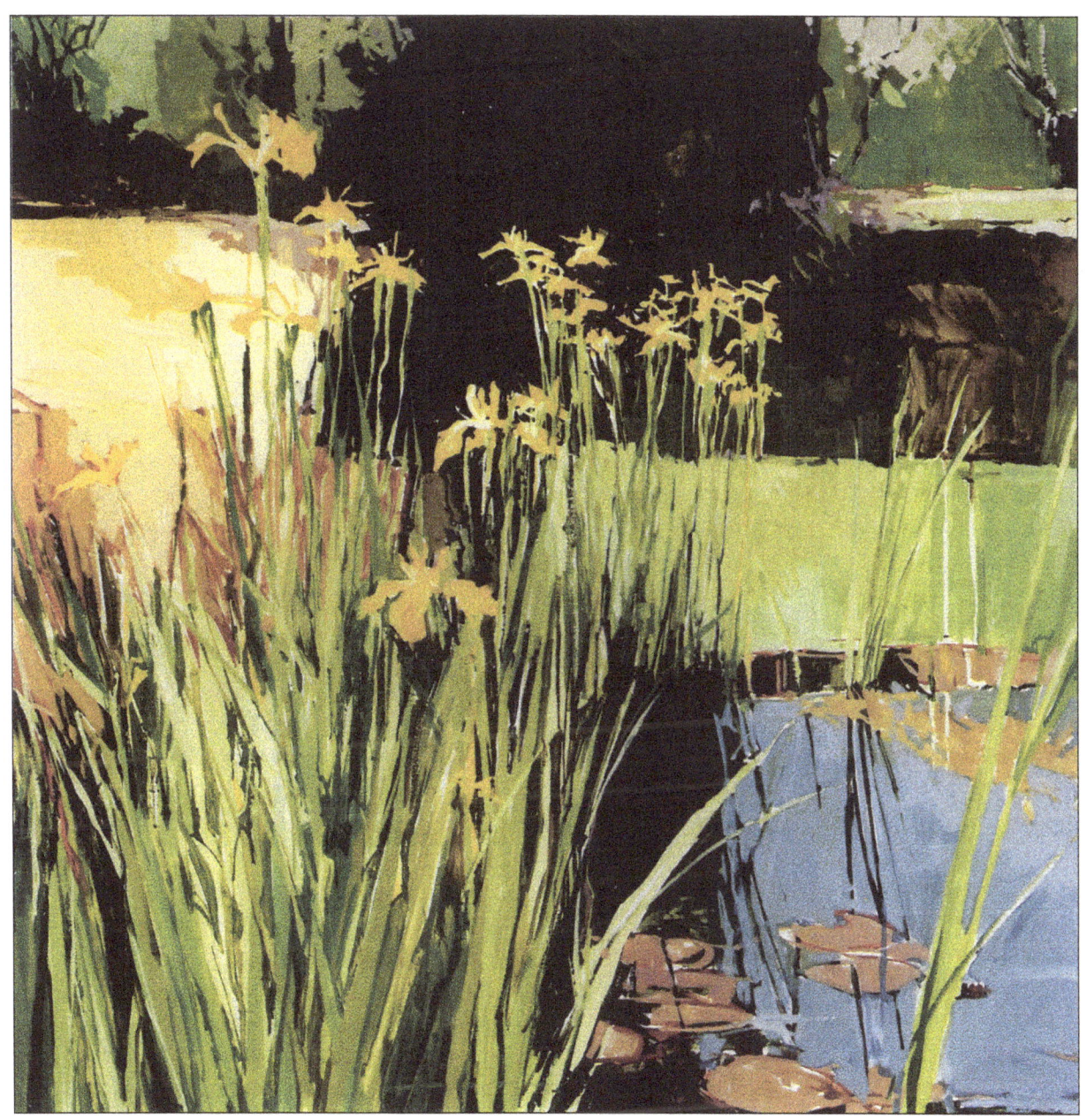

Galisteo Landscape/September (detail) *12x12 Acrylic on canvas*

This is a corner from a larger painting
that I repainted in a smaller format. I like to
find a section of a finished painting and
replicate it. It often gives a composition
that I would not have thought about
without it. I think I prefer
this detail version to the larger panel.

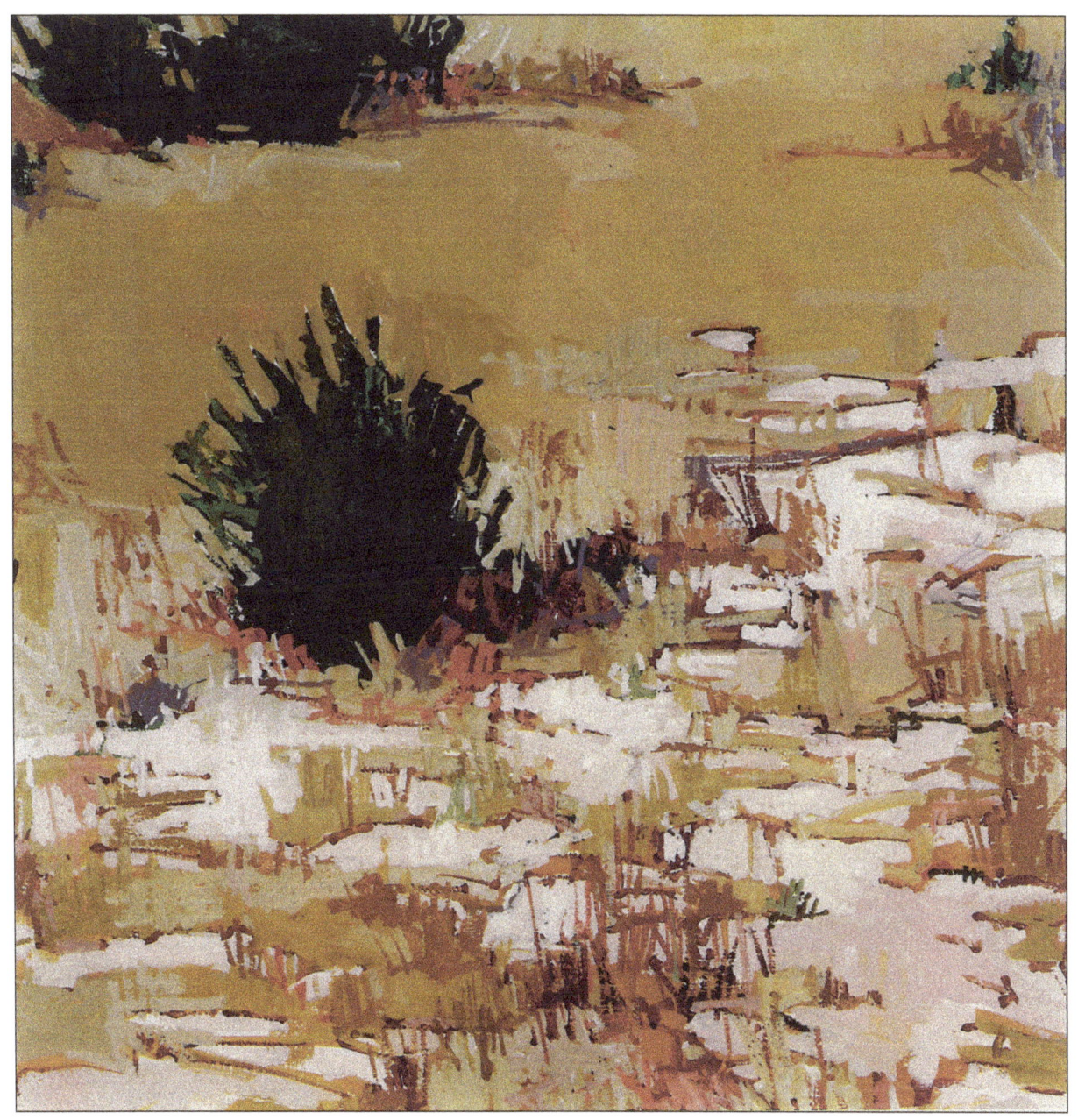

Date Palms Near Ouarzazate, Morocco *30x30 Acrylic on linen*

We had to ford this stream to get back to the
main road and I took a photo when
we slowed down. Morocco has so many colors
similar to New Mexico, with the addition
of date palm plantations. This was late May,
before all the green grasses turn to ochre.
The painting was done back in
my Santa Fe studio.

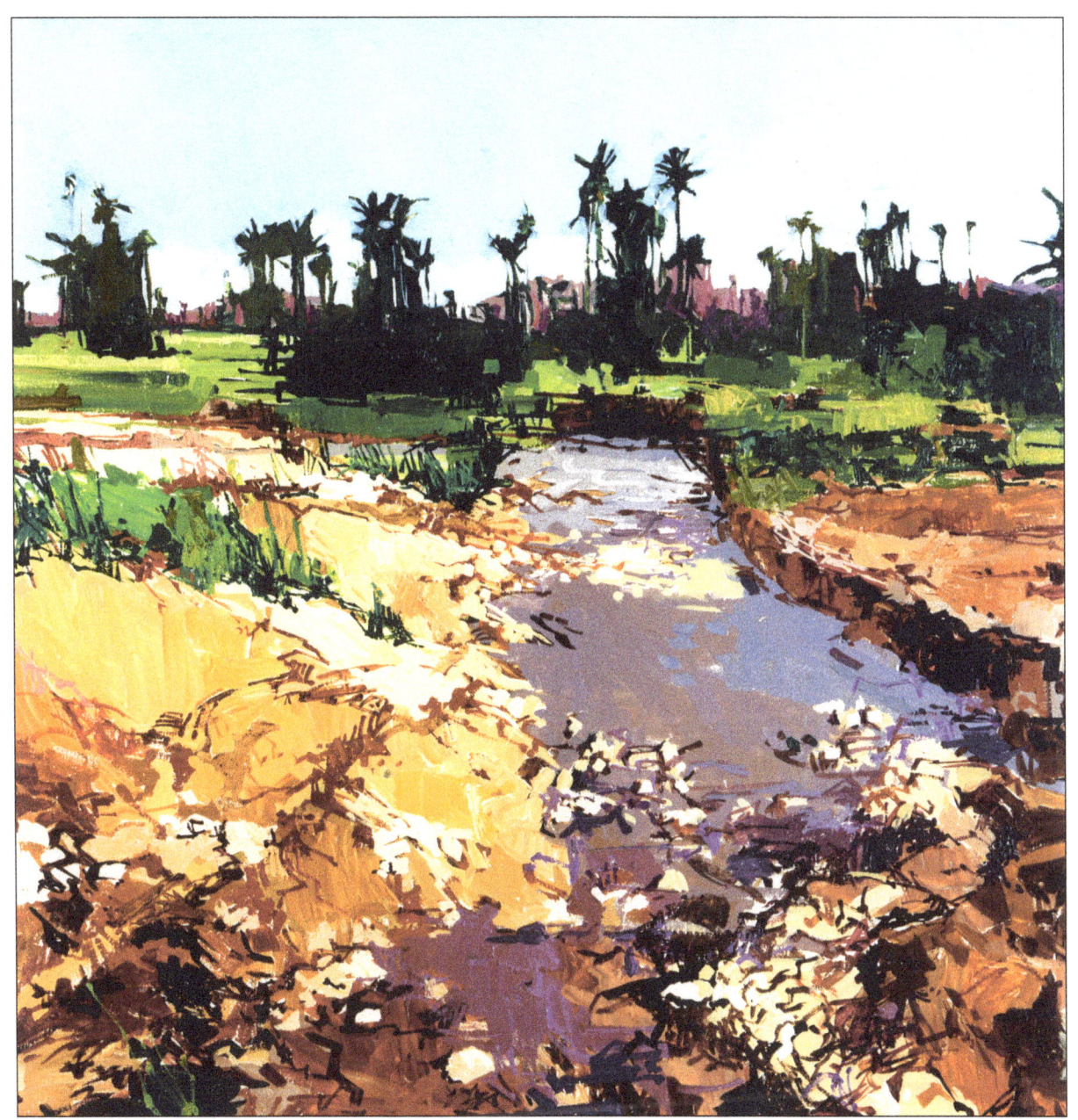

Black Mesa from the West *58x54 Acrylic on canvas*

A Tennessee couple saw a smaller version of
this scene and commissioned this larger piece.
Although the pueblo forbids it now,
Walter and I walked up to the top
for a fine view across the valley. It was a Super Bowl
Sunday and we suspected
that everyone in authority would be
fully distracted.

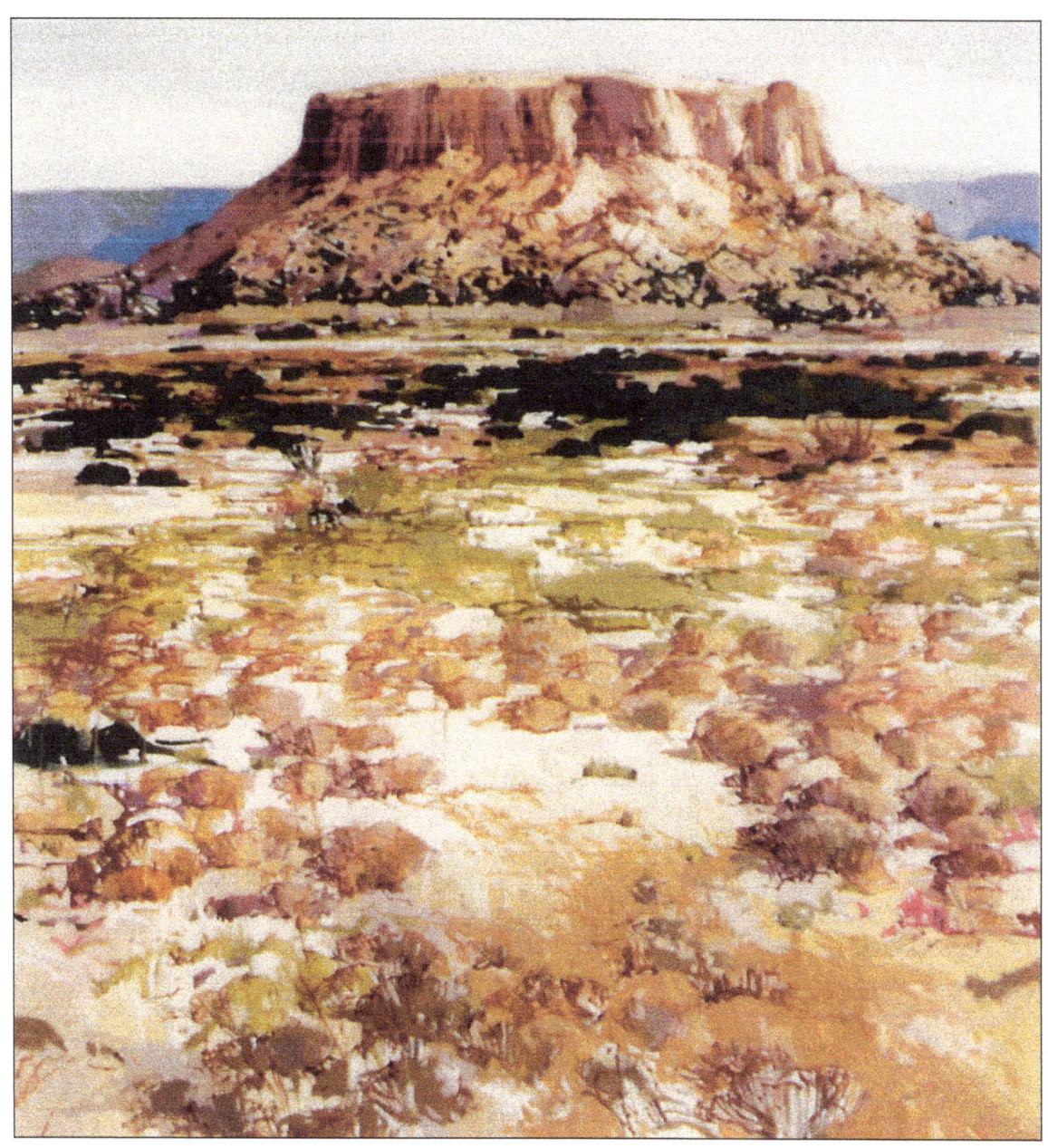

Winter Hillside, Galisteo *20x24 Acrylic on canvas*

There was a big snow in the year when I had
a studio in the village at Galisteo. This is
a scene from the south side of the creston
as the snow melts.
The studio was on land, two deeded lots, that
Betty Stewart and I bought from Jose Ortiz Y Pino.
We flipped a coin to see who got which lot, each
of us preferring the one with the stone walls
of a ruined farmhouse. Betty won.
When we started
to dig the footings for my adobe studio building, we
found a single man's patent leather dancing-slipper
just a foot down. And when we were planting the
trees in the garden, a skull emerged.
Galisteo remains a heady mix of enigmas.

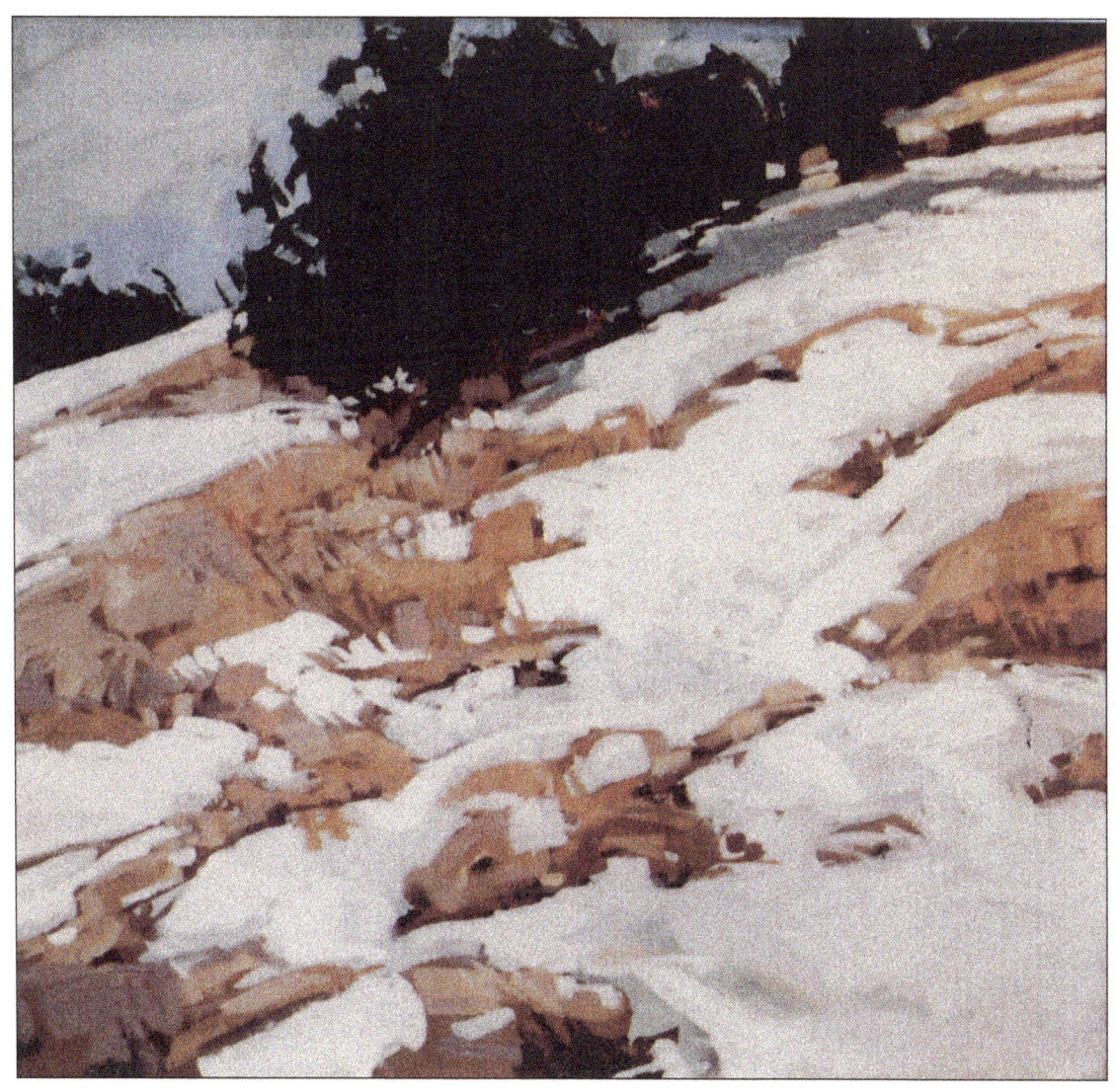

Late Winter Stream/Sangre de Cristos *32x30 Acrylic on canvas*

When the snow starts to thaw in the mountains,
sections of grass emerge from the mounds of white.
It is a favorite theme, graphic
elements of grass, water and snow.
It takes a bright sun to pull it
all together.

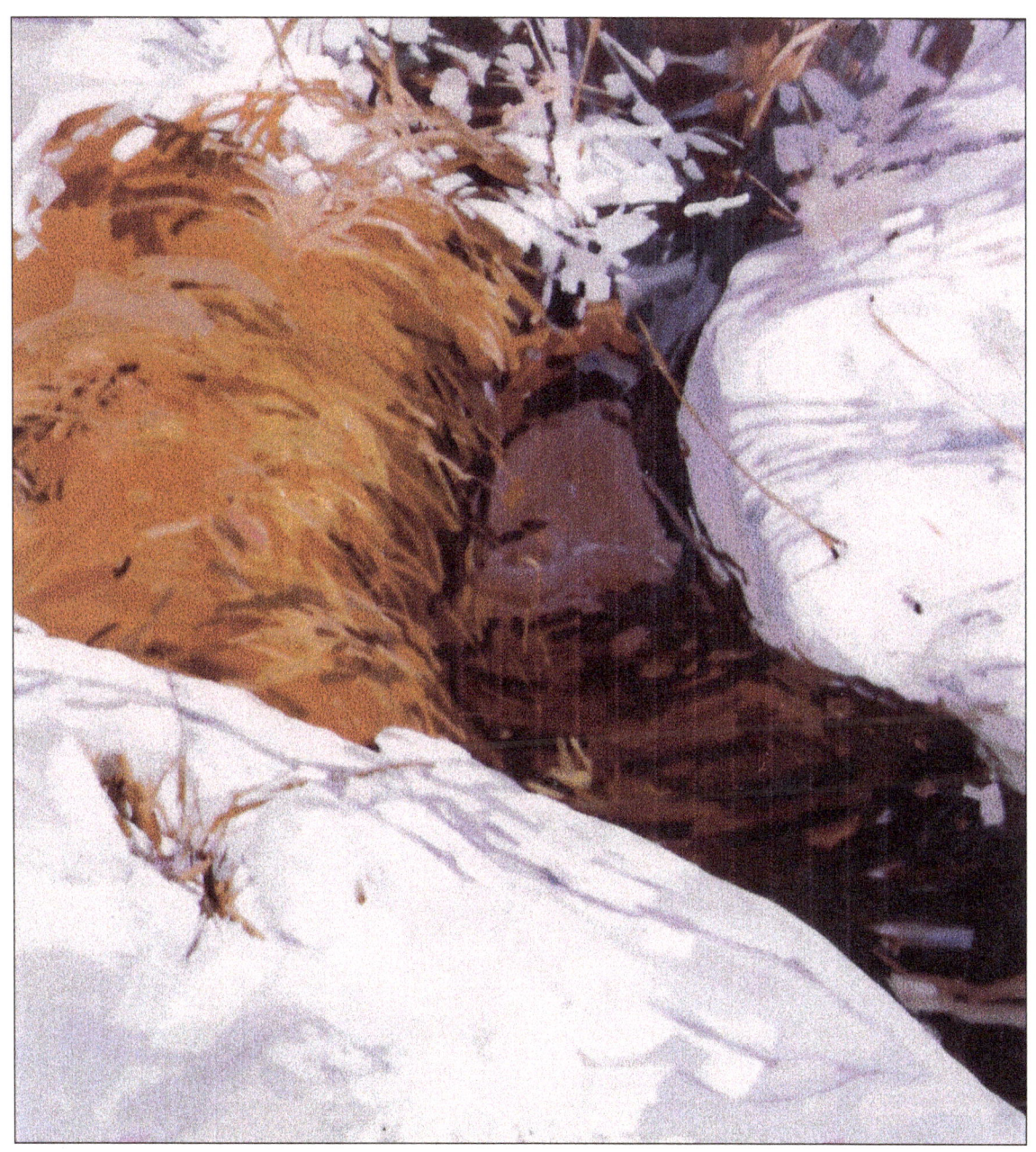

Cascade on the Big Tesuque *72x58 Acrylic on canvas*

And when the snow really starts to melt,
the surge of water in the Big Tesuque
makes wide waterfalls where a trickle
was before. This is a bold scene from
fairly high up the stream just before it
leads into the Aspen Meadows. I had trouble
convincing the German Shepherds
to stop playing in the water.

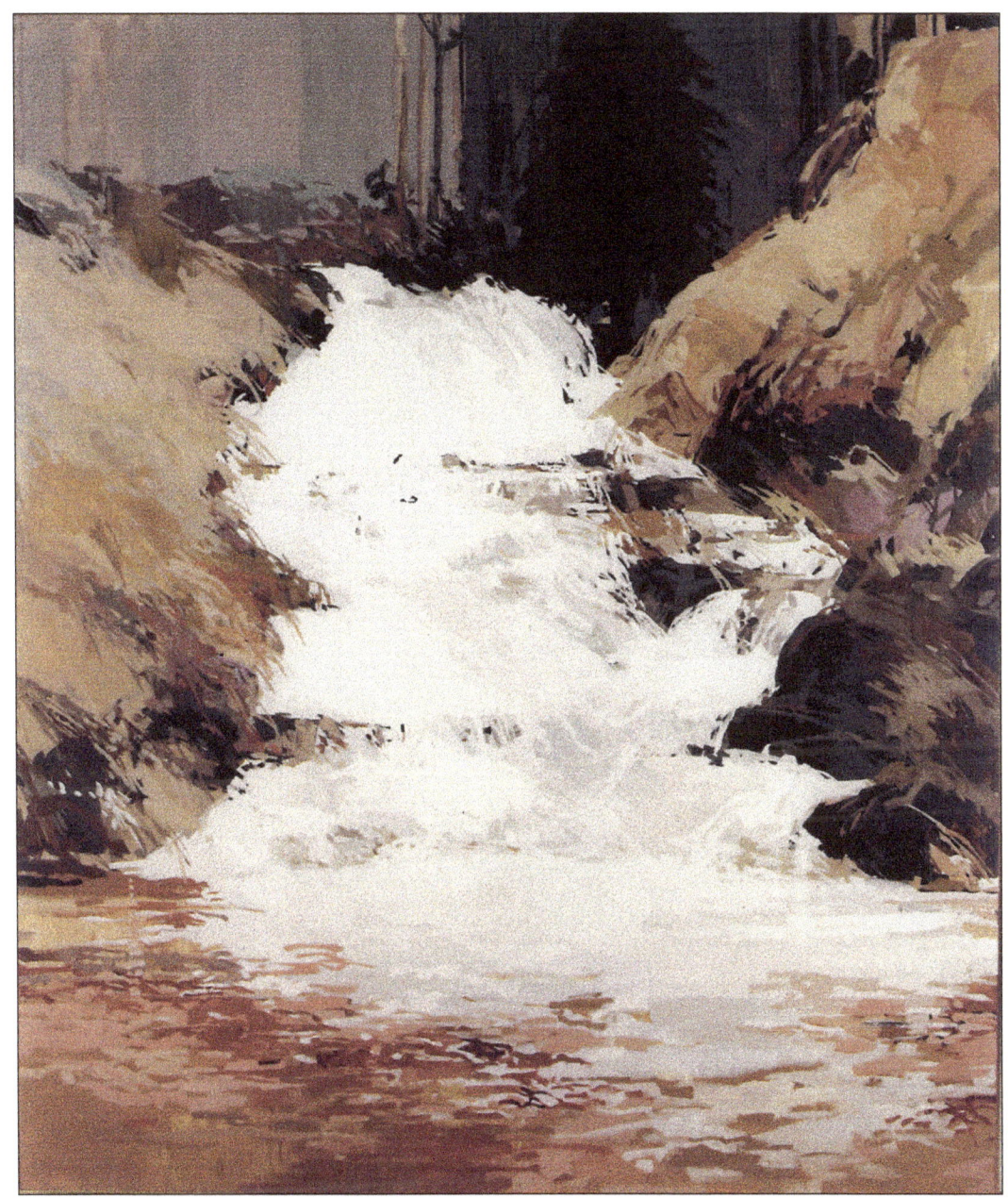

Fajada Butte V *24x16 Acrylic on canvas*

The national parks used to have a competition for
paintings of their parks, to be used in a calendar.
This is one of the four I submitted, none
of which won a mention. Chaco Canyon
remains a favorite motif, nonetheless.

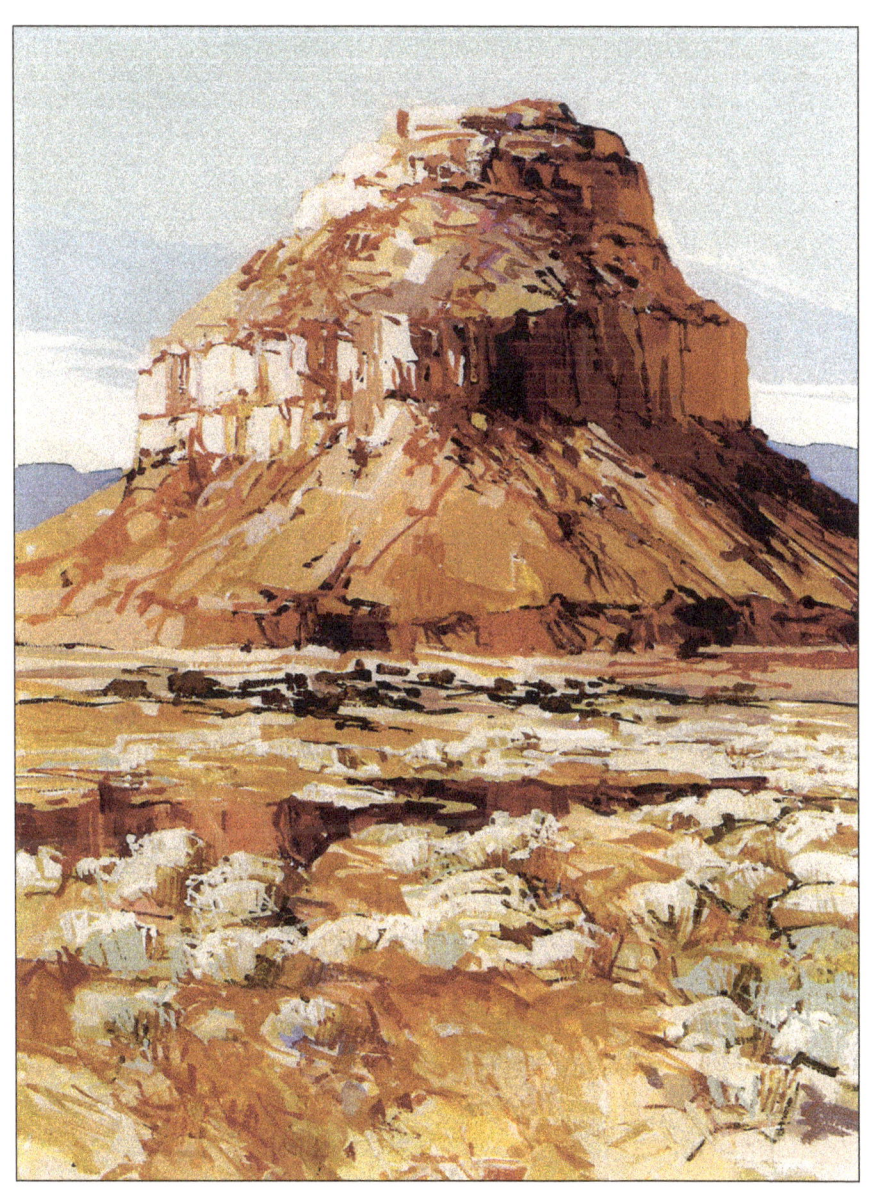

Canyon Road Apple *60x56 Acylic on canvas*

There aren't many of these grand old trees left along
Canyon Road now. This was painted fifteen years ago
when this one had a splendid bloom. In the 19th
century the property was an apple orchard and an apple
tree farm. It is all vacation houses and galleries now. Omer
and Bunny Claiborne have owned the property for many years,
the tree now only a tall stump. They have planted new trees,
crabapples and pears,
which may grow into such ultimate splendor.

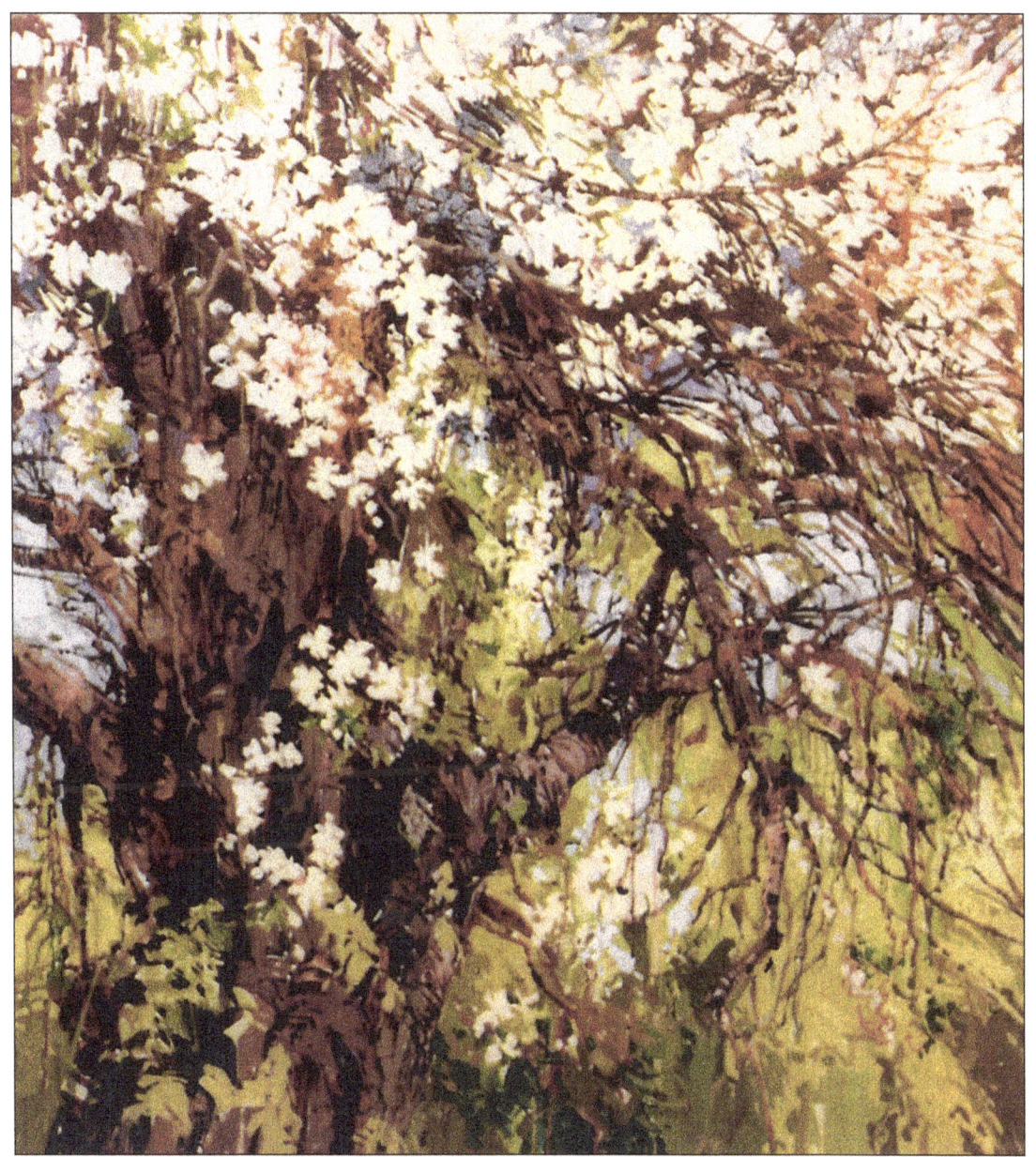

Poppies with Yellow Daisies, Studio Garden *40x40 Acrylic on linen*

A more complex rendering of this motif,
leaving pathways on both sides of the border.
I combined a spring scene with the
Flanders poppies that usually come later.
Packets of poppy seeds contain thousands of
seeds, but I can get only a few to germinate.

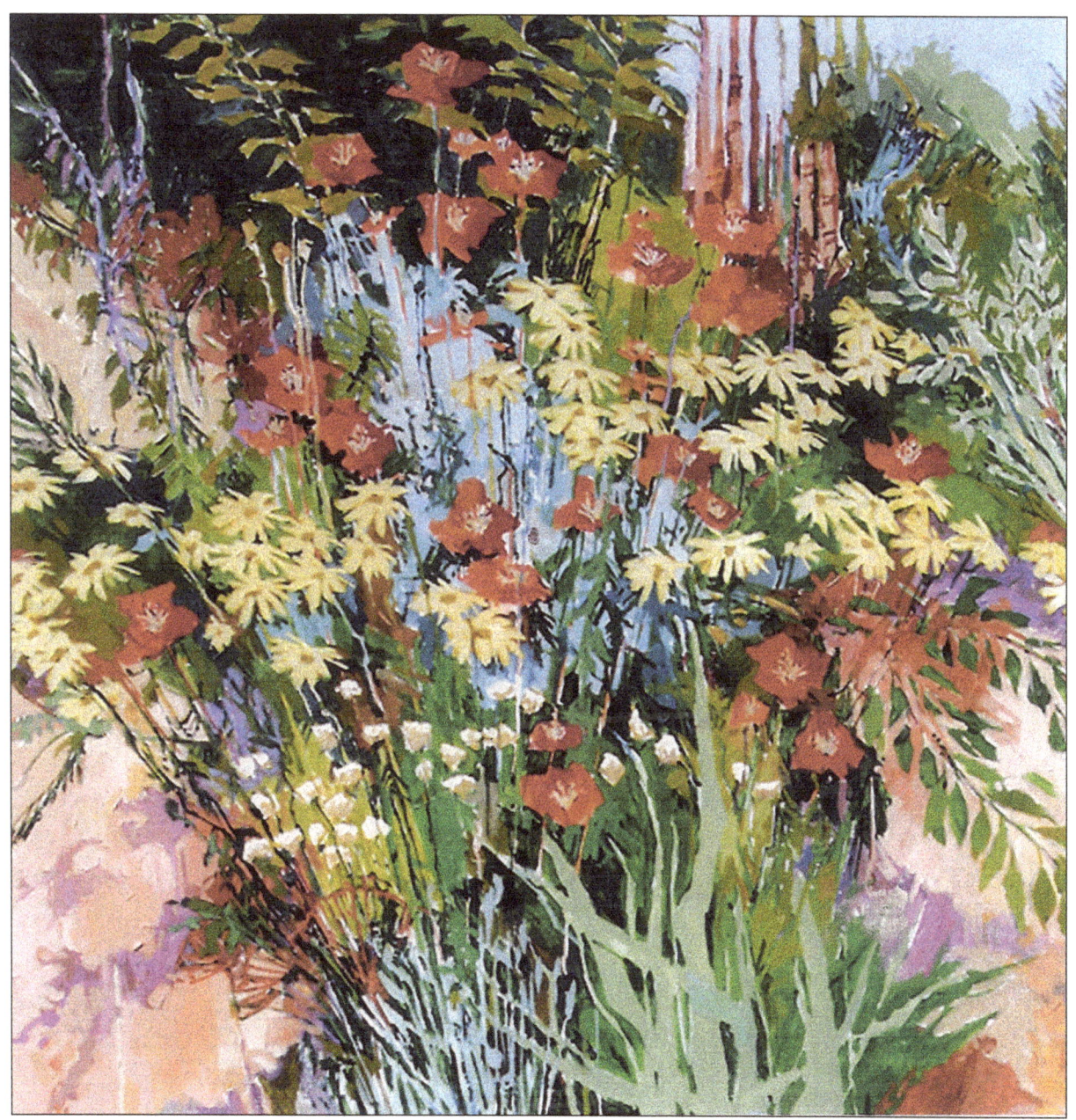

Southview/Galisteo *44x44 Acrylic on linen*

This is the first of a series of four views looking
south from the house in Ranchitos de Galisteo.
A late summer version with green grasses from
August rains. I painted several small versions
out on a French easel but this one
came from work in the studio. No winds
to topple the easel or no‑see‑ums to buzz
around and bite.

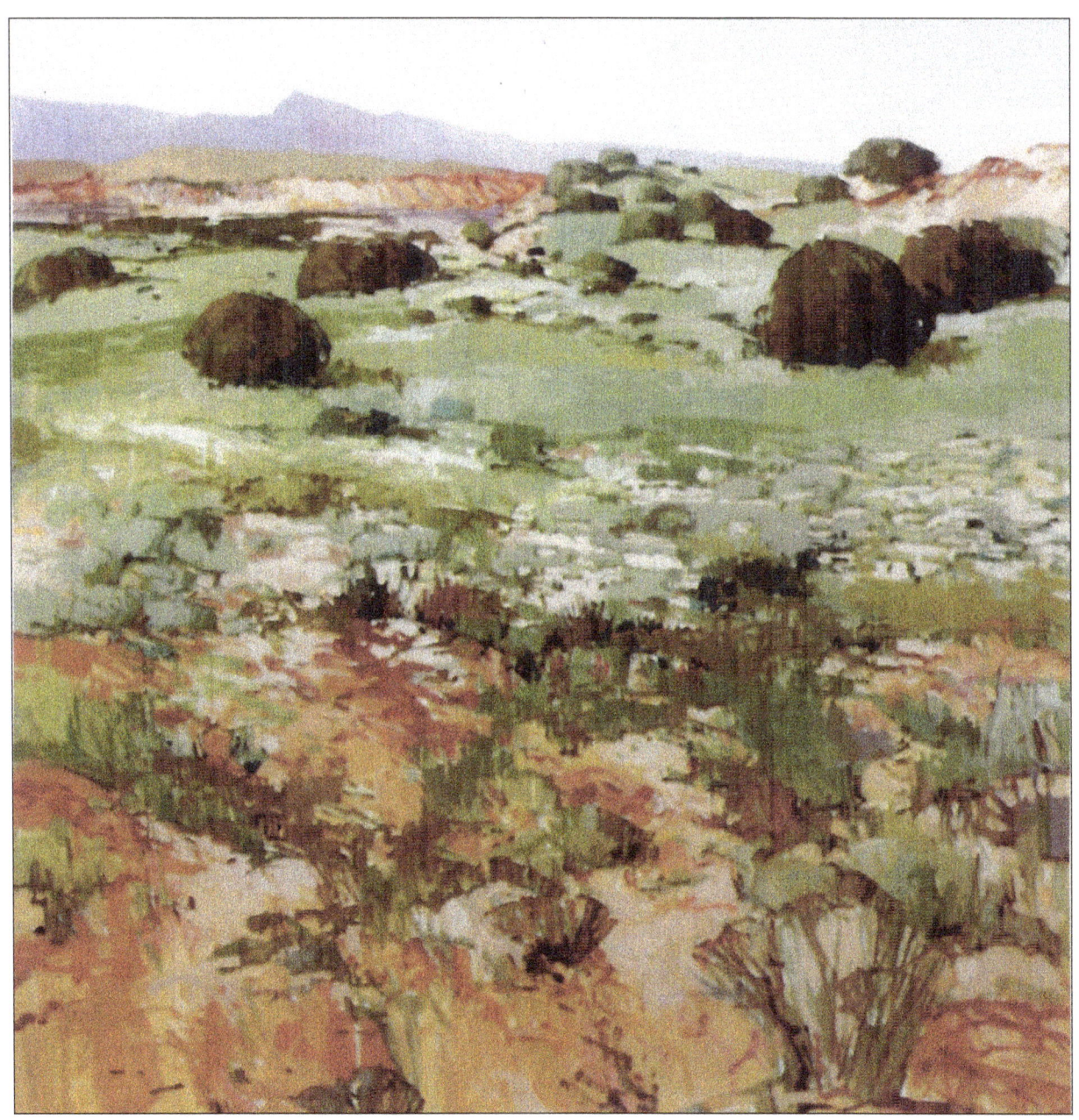

Sangre Cascade, Big Tesuque *72x40 Acrylic on linen*

I liked the verticality of this scene, the trees a balance
for the water. This painting sat for years in my studio
until I decided to cut off the bottom fifth
of the canvas. I had it reframed and
immediately people began to
notice it. Put your hand across the bottom
cascade to see what it looks like now.

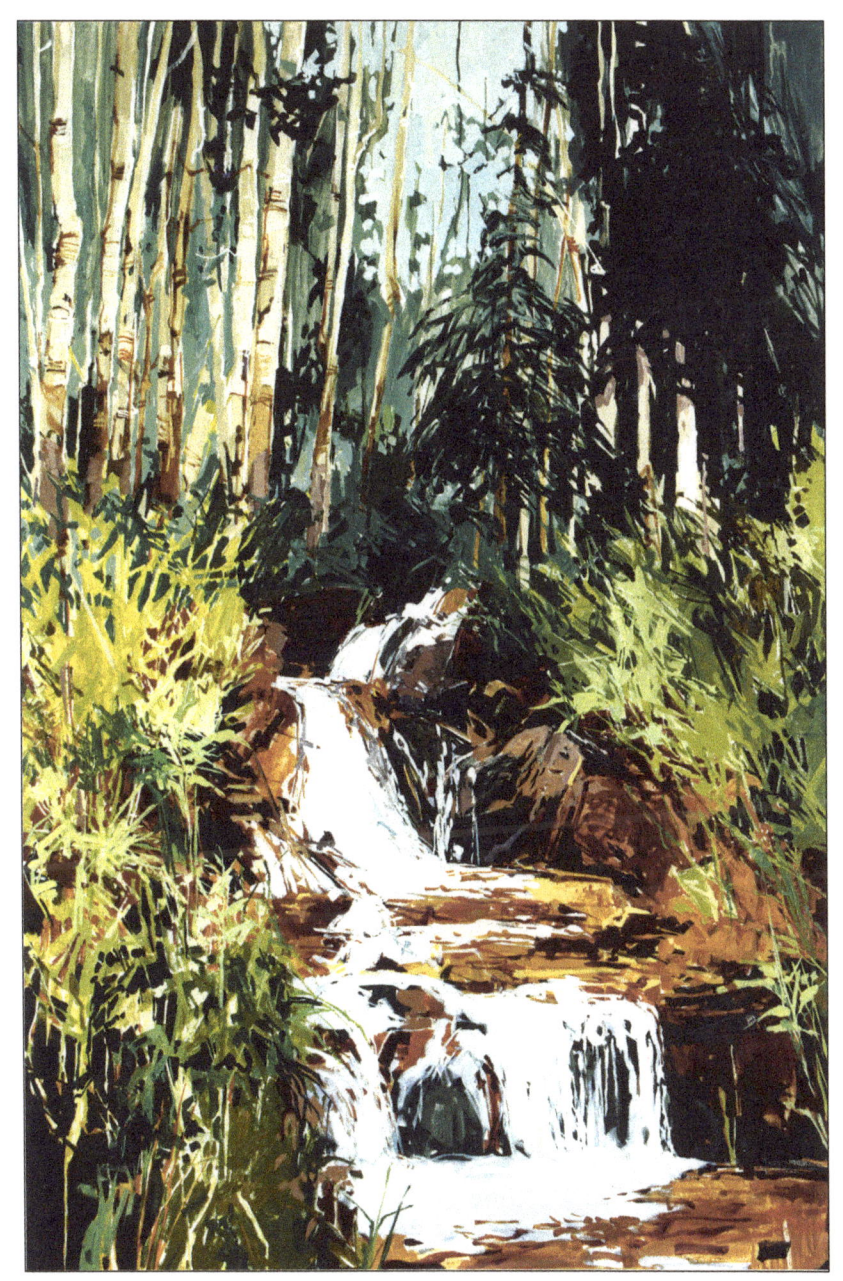

Studio Garden with Anthemis & Daylily *32x32 Acrylic on linen*

The studio garden without the
bright reds that usually abound there.
By now the latilla fence in the upper right
is almost a signature because all my gardens
are enclosed in a fence like that. The fence
indicates to me that this is a New Mexico garden.
The path in the lower left gives
some geometry
to the scene, angles to fight with
the foliage.

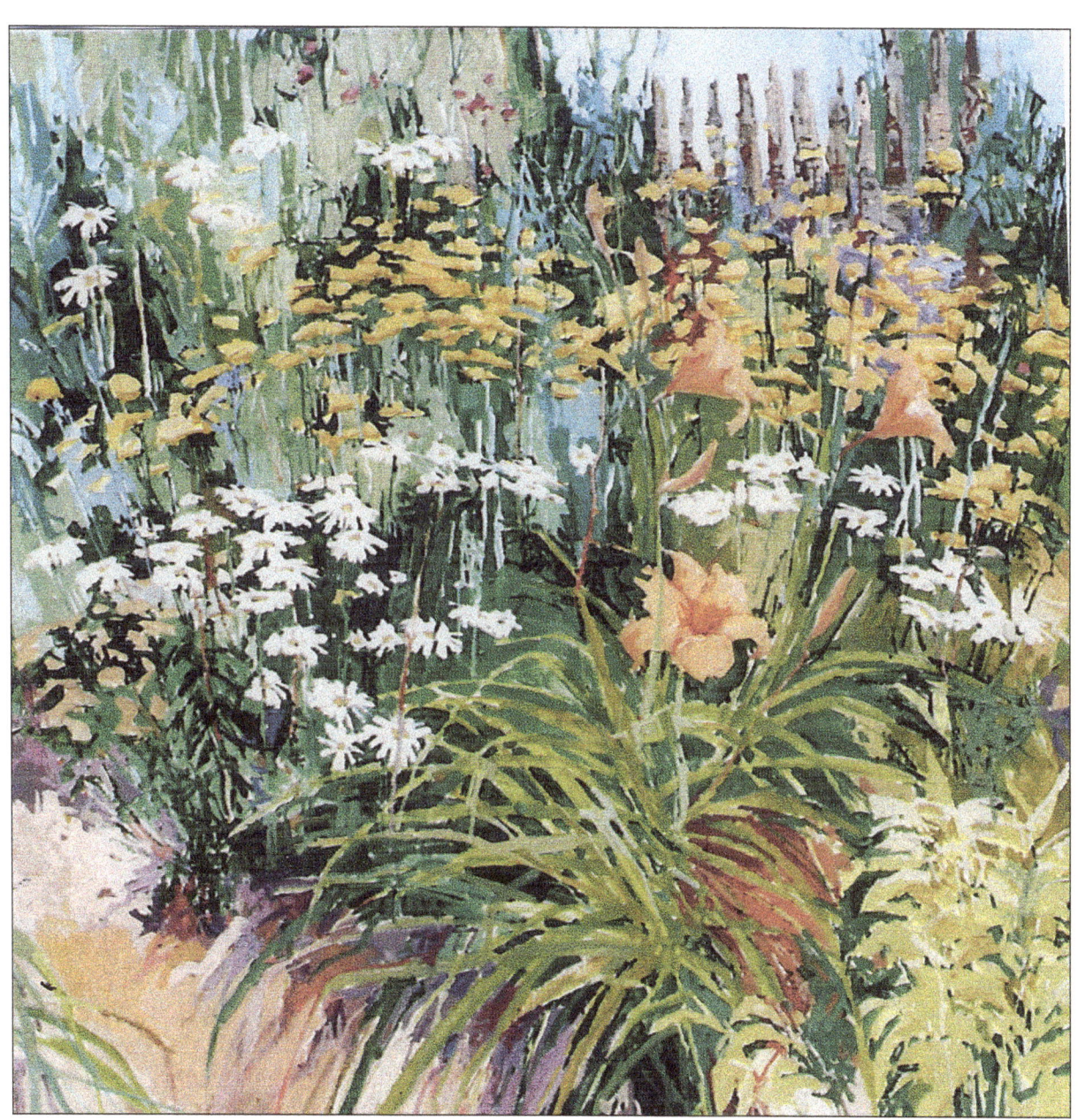

Back Garden with Tulips *30x30 Acrylic on canvas*

I don't know why I do not paint tulips more often
as I have plenty of them in my gardens. Perhaps
I am painting winter landscapes while they are in bloom.
I did manage to get this one completed
before the last petal fell. I noticed some new gopher
holes in the studio terrace at Fort Union Drive,
so I better get going. Gophers love tulips.

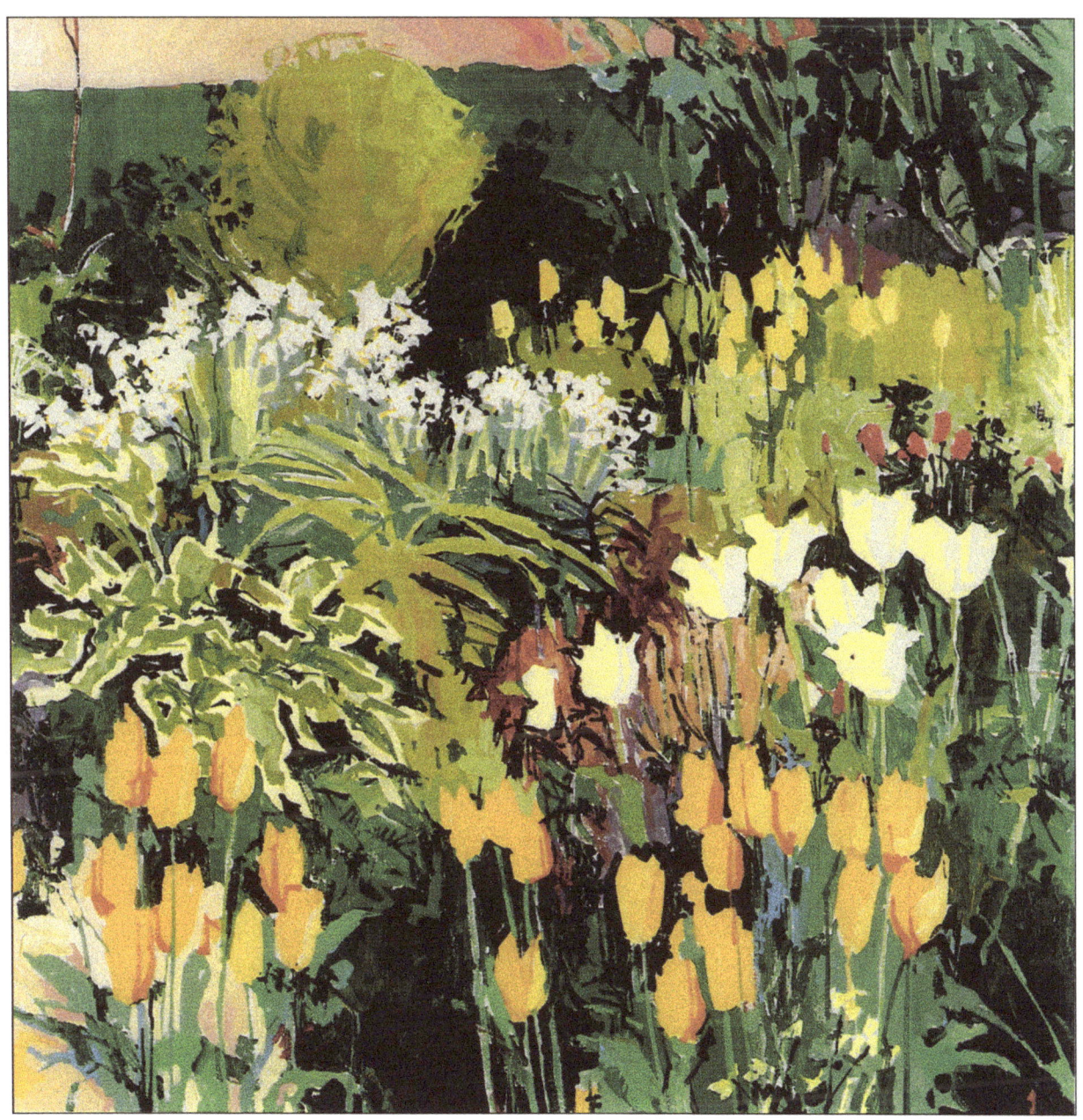

White Poppies and Anthemis *58x54 Acrylic on canvas*

For a short while I had white opium poppies
reseeding in a former studio garden and there is
no more handsome poppy. Agua Fria Nursery
usually has a flat or two of them in the spring, under the
Latin name *Papaver somniferum.* The plants could
be grown for the striking green seed⁄pods alone. Anthemis
and the usual suspects filled out this garden.

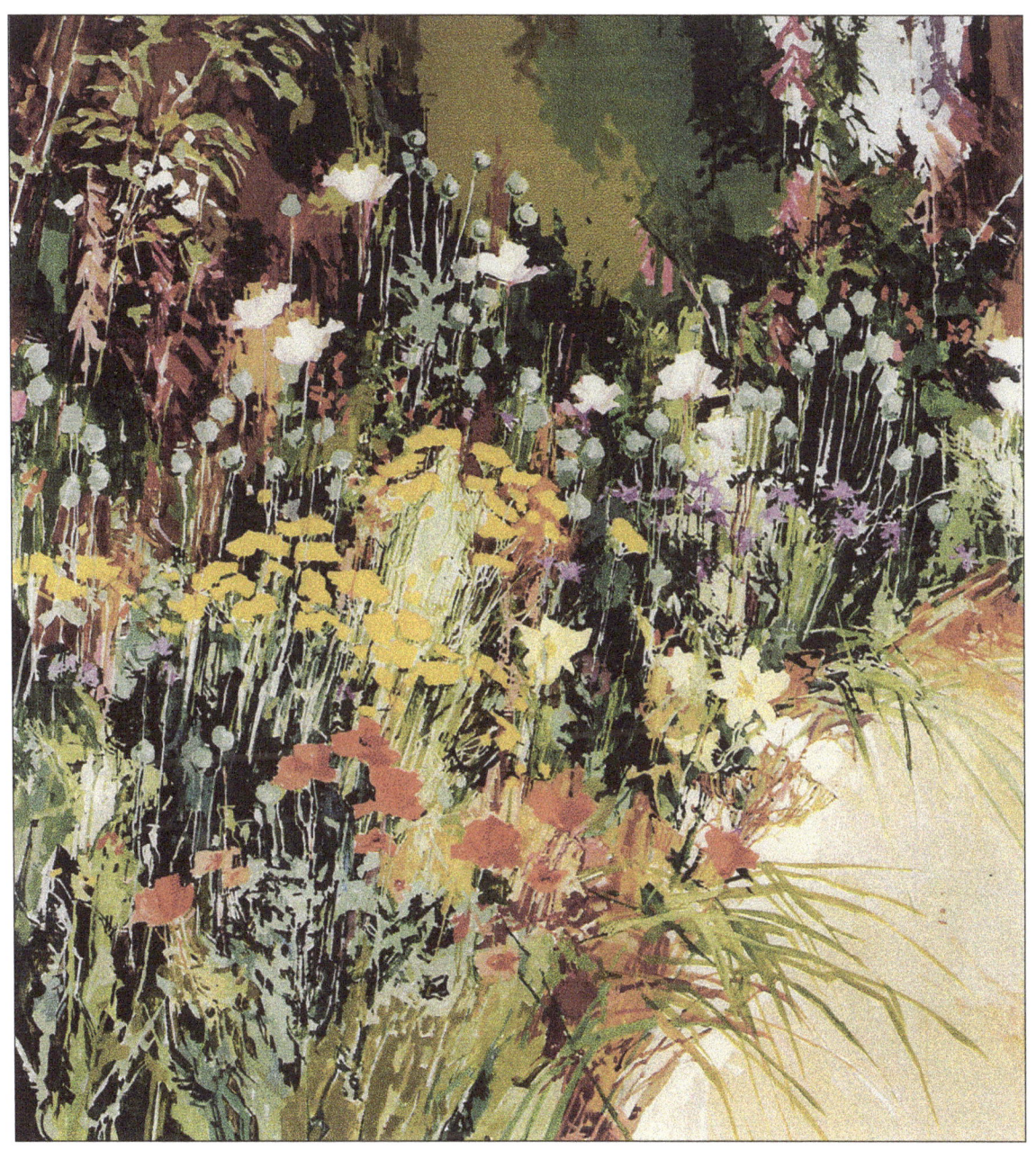

Garden View, Yellow and White *58x54 Acrylic on canvas*

I liked this corner of the English garden, with
just a hint of a grey stone column and urn
in the upper right. The strong yellow
band of yarrow gives the garden an informal
center. Would that I could grow a garden
this fulsome. The New York Graphic Society
has done a grand poster of this painting.

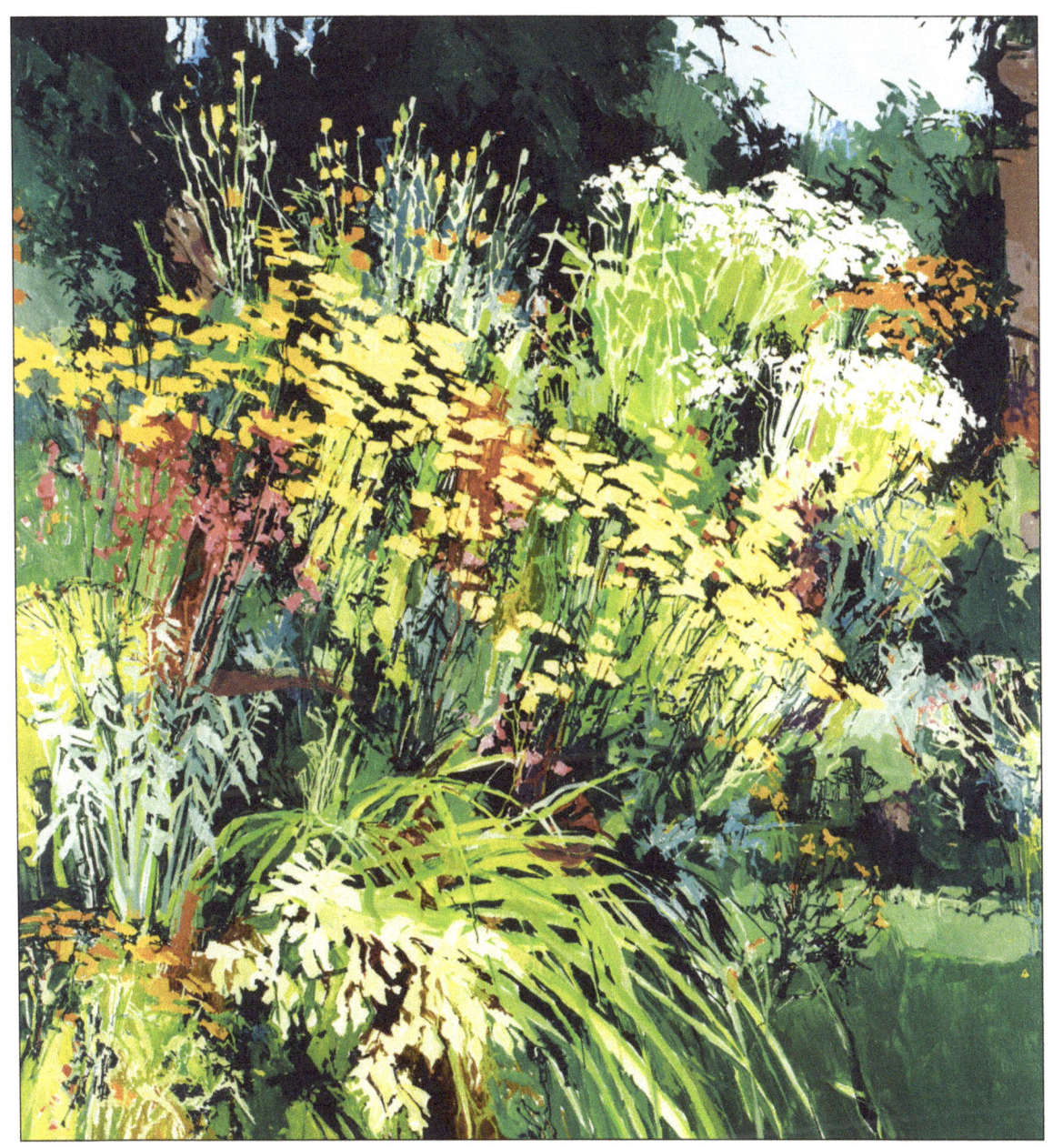

White Stucco House near Moroccan Village, *30x30 Acrylic on canvas*

Driving south out of Tangier, we passed this
small house across from a distant white village.
I snapped a photo out of the moving car,
nearly in focus. This was the first painting
I completed on my return to the Santa Fe studio.
The green fields looked more like Italy or Spain, but
it was the green Morocco that resulted from a
notably wet winter. Fields of red poppies
would come into view just around the bend.

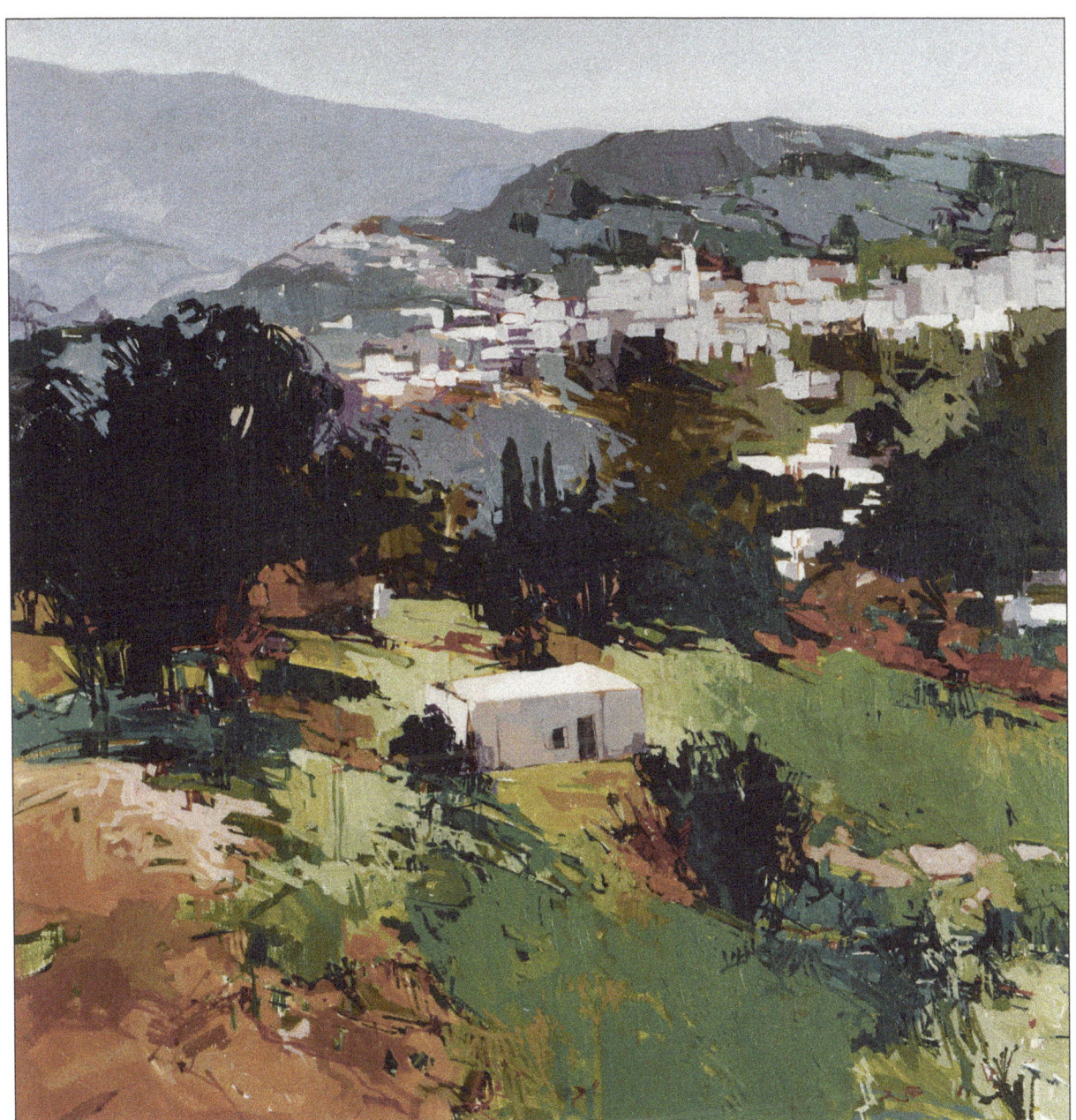

Abiquiu Mesa, Night *32x32 Acrylic on linen*

In some ways I prefer this sombre black-and-white
version from the mesa series. I mixed the blacks from
burnt umber and ultramarine, so it varies in
hue with warmer bits in the middle. And
the shapes became stronger without the distraction
of reds and siennas.

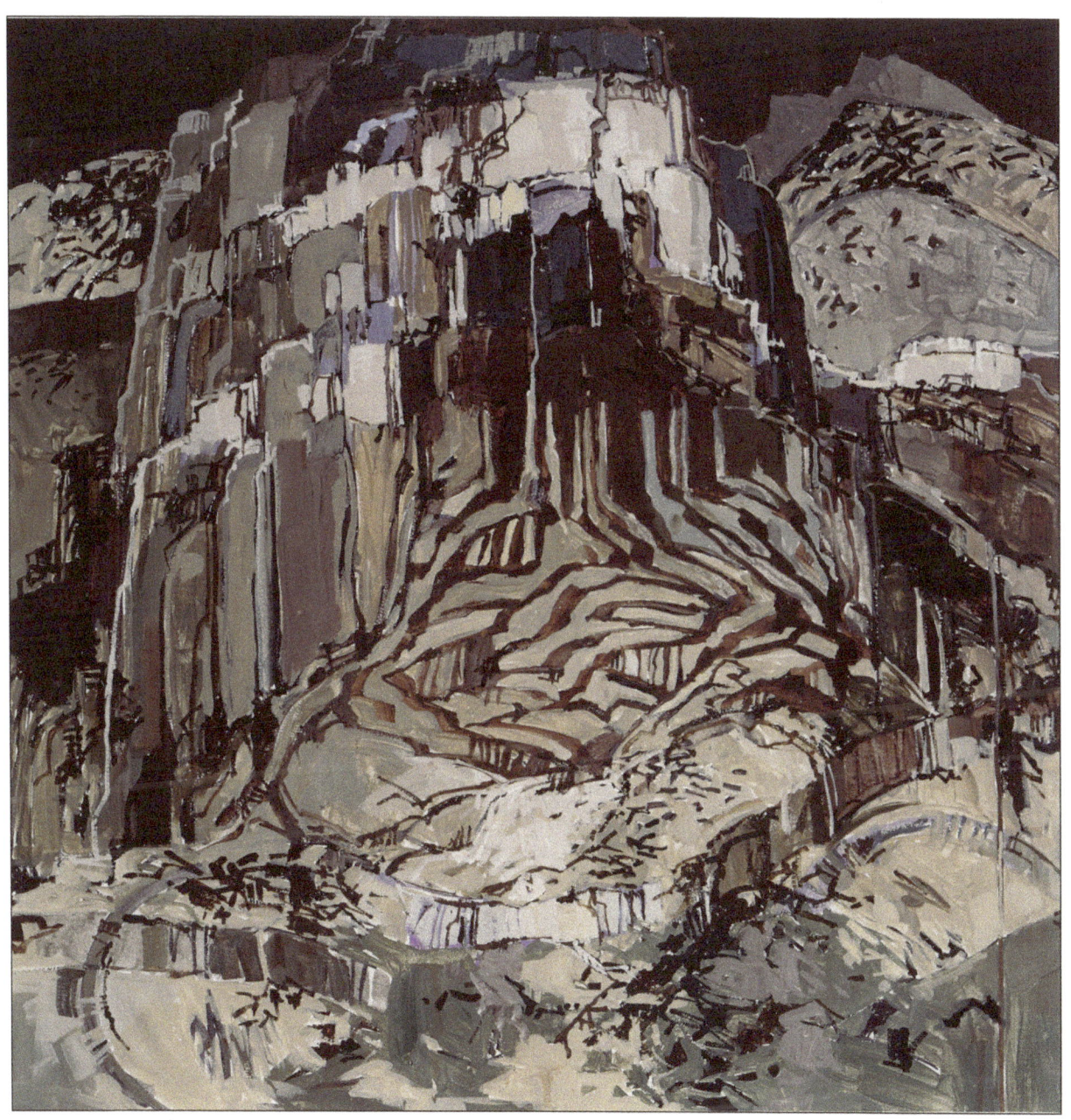

Black Canyon II *30x30 Acrylic on linen canvas*

A darker version of the canyon, from a slightly elevated
point of view. Although it is a view seen from the edge
of the canyon, I tried to make it as if the viewer
was hovering thirty feet or so highter.
Wagner was again being broadcast from
the Metropolitan Opera and who elose could
write theme music for this canyon?

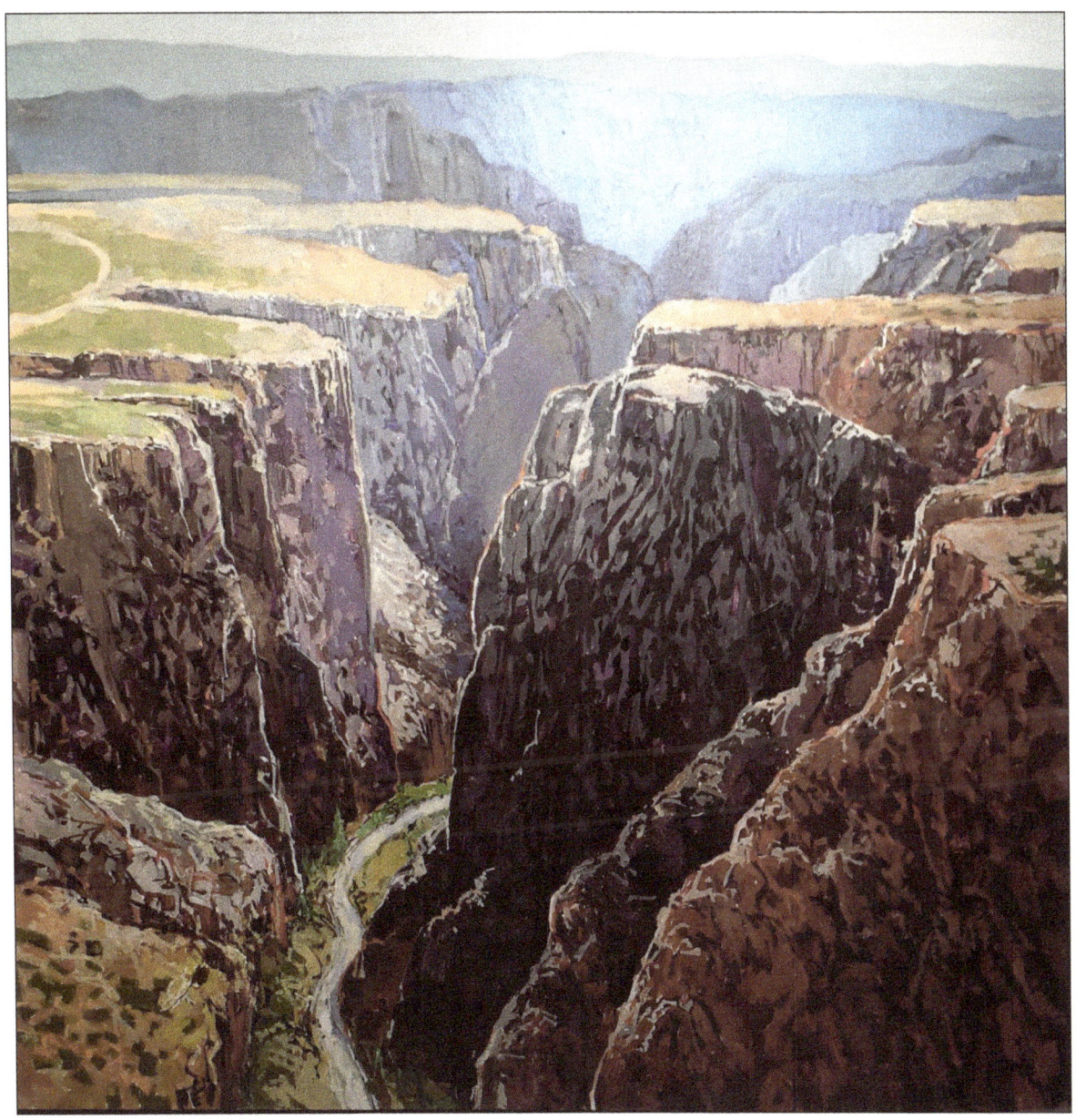

Yellow Iris, Fort Union Drive Garden *30x24 Acrylic on linen*

An enthusiastic group of yellow iris bloomed
quite well in the back garden. The next year
they seemed to have disappeared entirely, so I was
fortunate to get this painting. Iris have a short
number of years to show their stuff, then they
need to be divided and planted elsewhere.
They are worth the effort.

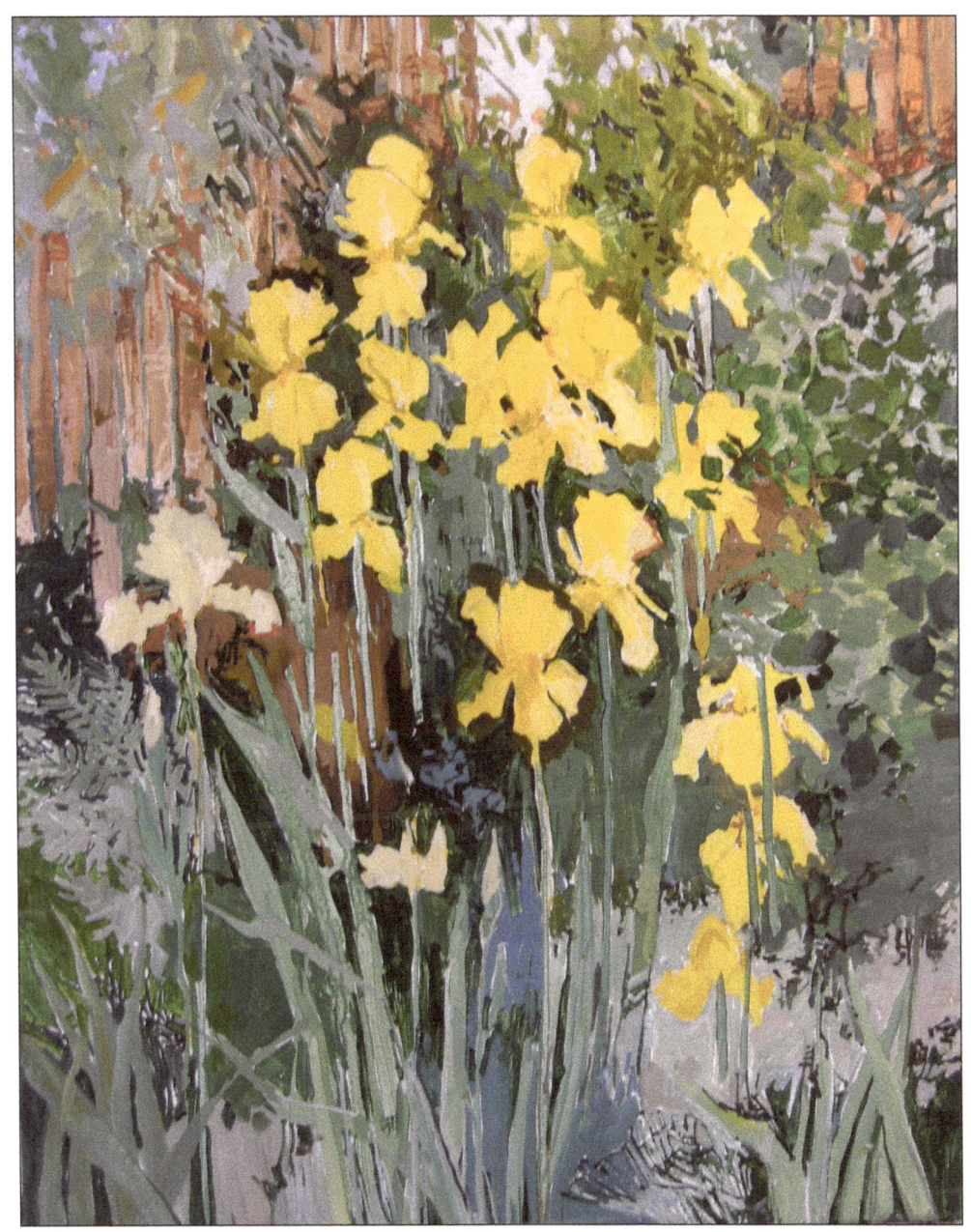

Studio on Fort Union Drive

This was a good studio for me, light
coming in from two sides and a skylight
right over the easel. A flower garden was
just outside of the south doors and I could go outside
as the painting progressed to check on colors or
to revisit how a branch looked. My new studio
on Cristobal Lane
is planned with the same mix of bluish north
light, warm south light and the blush from a skylight.
I also plan to have the ceiling supported by
exposed trusses painted white.
The floors will be bricks taken up from Agnes Sims'
house on Canyon Road, the current owner
preferring to pour a new floor of solid concrete.

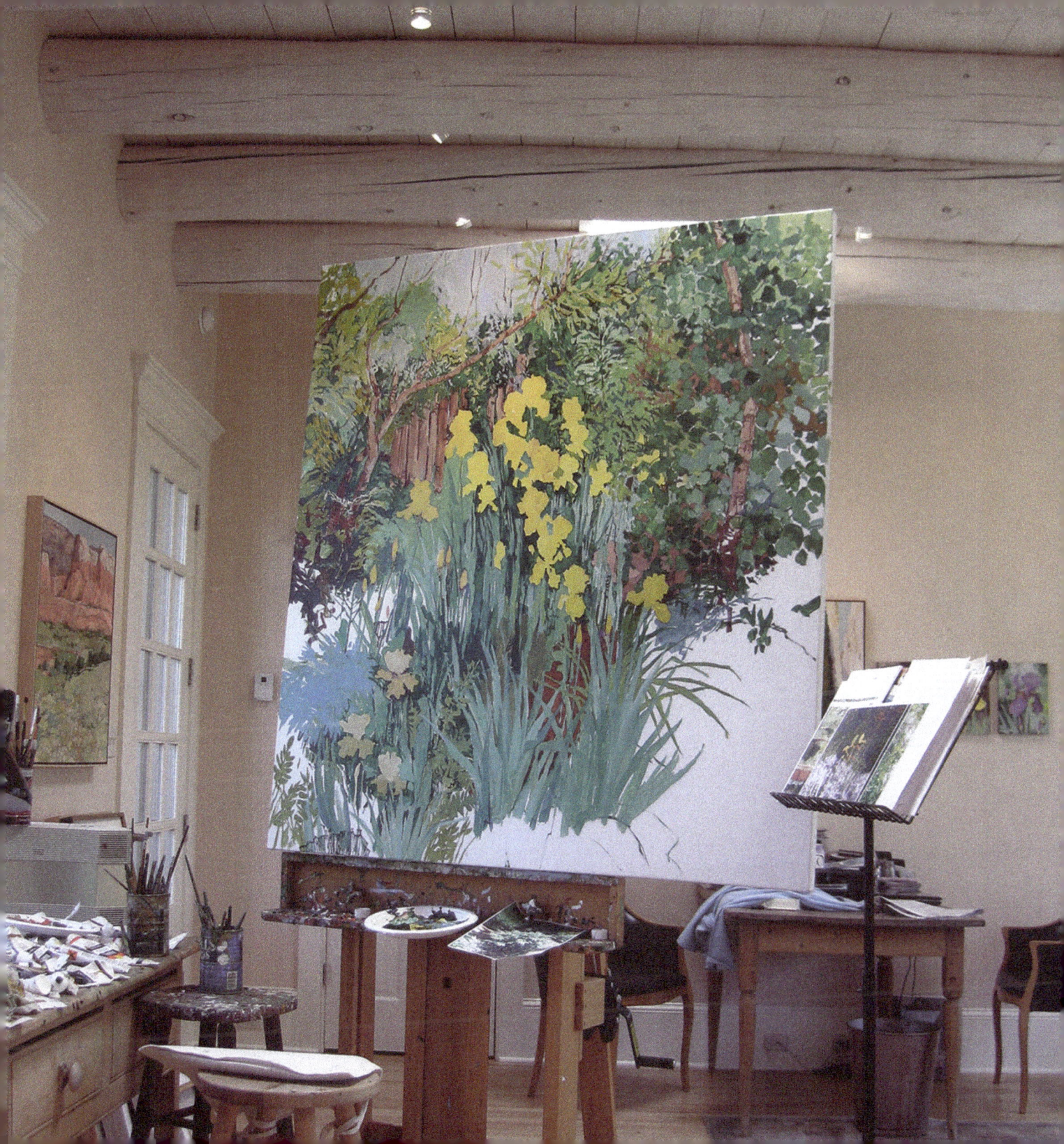

The typeface of this book is set in Poliphilus, cast
from English monotype matrices. Poliphilus had its origin in the
singlularly beautitul roman type cut by Francesco da Bologna for the
Hypnerotomachia Poliphili, issued in 1499 by Aldus Manutius (1450–1515).